SO-BRQ-949

DATE DUE

MAR 1 2 2001

MAY 2 2 2001

OCT 2 0 2010

DEMCO, INC. 38-2931

Renner Learning Resource Center
Elgin Community College
Elgin, IL 60123

Acknowledgments

I extend deep gratitude to the girls and women who shared their perspectives about black women and hair. They are the true authors of *Hair Matters*. Many thanks to those who helped me recruit girls and women, and to all those who allowed me to take their photos.

I am thankful to many individuals for their support during various stages of the project. Thanks go to Jose Saldívar, Norma Alarcón, Nancy Chodorow, and Michael Omi for believing in the project during its earliest stages. They were indeed a "dream team" dissertation committee at the University of California, Berkeley, and I am forever grateful for their support. Thanks also go to Sonja Peterson-Lewis, Vèvè Clark, and JoAnn Intilli for providing equal amounts of support and critical feedback during the early stages of the project. I am also grateful to Pedro Noguera for his support as I put together my dissertation committee. Many thanks to Danielle Percy and Kathleen Wager for administrative support as the book came to a close.

I was fortunate to receive a dissertation fellowship at the Center for Black Studies at the University of California, Santa Barbara, during the academic year 1996–1997. While there, I was also a visiting lecturer in the Department of Sociology. During that time, I met two scholars who became wonderful mentors and friends—a very special thanks to Claudine Michel and Kum-Kum Bhavnani for their never-ending support and enthusiasm for the project and for providing critical feedback for my earlier writings. Thanks also go to Cynthia Hudley, Bill Bielby, Harvey

x   Molotch, and Marti Adams, as well as to the members of the Center for Black Studies and the Department of Sociology.

I have been blessed with wonderful friends who supported me in many ways during various stages of preparing *Hair Matters:* Karyn Lacy, Sara Johnson, Tracy Johnson, Karolyn Tyson, Jelani Mahiri, Lynnea Stephen, Nicole Thandiwe Atkinson, Marshelle Jones, Felicia Law, Ford Hatamiya, Celsa Snead, Tammy Dowley-Blackman, Mark Blackman, Marcus Green, Beverly Bunch-Lyons, Susan Gooden, Gretchen Givens, Mike Herndon, P. S. Polanah, and Maria Franklin.

During the last year of writing the book, many friends and colleagues helped me tremendously and I am thankful for their support and critical feedback as the writing came to an end. Many thanks to Martha McCaughey for reading the Introduction and providing critical feedback. Thanks to Stacey Floyd-Thomas and Juan Floyd-Thomas for helping me organize my thoughts. A very special thanks to France Winddance Twine and Jonathan Warren for opening up their home and work space to me in Seattle two weeks before the deadline of the manuscript in late December 1998. Their support of the project and critical feedback on the "Black Expectations" section of Appendix I was invaluable. A very big thanks to Niko Pfund and his staff at New York University Press. Niko's excitement, support, and feedback as I completed *Hair Matters* were extraordinary. A very big thanks to Despina Papazoglou Gimbel at New York University Press for support during the final stages of the book.

Last but not least, much love and thanks go to Grace Carroll, Julana Massey, Tajai Massey, Lorraine Caldwell, and the whole Carroll clan. Over the years they have provided me with a family space that has nurtured my personal and intellectual growth.

Introduction

Unhappy to Be Nappy

In late November 1998, Ruth Sherman, a white teacher at predominantly black and Hispanic Public School (P.S.) 75 in Brooklyn, found herself embroiled in a national controversy after using Carolivia Herron's children's book *Nappy Hair* (1997) in her third-grade class. The story's main character, Brenda, has long and "kinky" or "nappy" hair. Blacks use these words to describe black hair that is tightly coiled or curled in texture. But "nappy" is historically a derogatory term. Although many blacks embraced nappy, or natural, hair in the late 1960s and early 1970s, some still perceived the term, and the hair, negatively.

Nappy hair could not escape its history. Although natural hairstyles made a comeback in the 1990s, some black Brooklyn residents living near P.S. 75 felt the book was inappropriate because of the reference to nappy hair. According to newspaper reports, a black parent, Cathy Wright, found photocopied pages of the story in one of her daughter's school folders. Soon several other adults, most of whom were not parents of children at P.S. 75, were complaining about the use of the story. Once the story made national news, Herron, an assistant professor of English at California State University at Chico, made it clear that her story was indeed *a celebration* of nappy or kinky hair. She was targeting the very kids that attend P.S. 75 as her audience. However, instead of viewing Herron's work in the spirit that it was written, the protesters viewed Ms. Sherman's use of the story as offensive and derogatory. According to the *New York Times,* even after hearing Herron's motive in writing *Nappy Hair,* Ms. Wright explained that the story "did not make her feel good as a black woman and did not make her daughter feel good about herself."

The case vividly demonstrates the tensions that surface in black communities when it comes to hair. Hair matters in black communities, and it matters in different ways for women and men. For black women in this society, what is considered desirable and undesirable hair is based on one's hair texture. What is deemed desirable is measured against white standards of beauty, which include long and straight hair (usually blonde), that is, hair that is not kinky or nappy. Consequently, black women's hair, in general, fits outside of what is considered desirable in mainstream society. Within black communities, straighter variety and texture are privileged as well. Such hair is described as "good," while nappy hair like Brenda's is "bad." Therefore, the kinky and nappy hair that Herron celebrates in her story goes uncelebrated among a race of people still nursing the wounds of slavery.

But what if Ms. Sherman had been black? Would her actions have been met with the same protest? Who is allowed to address issues that are particular to black communities? After all, Ms. Sherman was using a book written by a black woman to teach black and Hispanic kids that "black is beautiful." Still, at a community meeting in downtown Brooklyn attended by Herron shortly after Ms. Sherman was reprimanded, Carlos Bristol, a local black resident, questioned the ability of a white teacher to provide a historical context for "nappy hair." In addition, how, he wondered, could a white teacher use and appropriate the term in such a way that she could explain to black kids that nappy hair is beautiful? An important and debatable point, surely, but given the reaction to Herron's story among some blacks and given how black people reinforce hierarchies based on hair and skin color, one might ask if a black person, simply by virtue of his or her skin color, could provide a nuanced account of *Nappy Hair*? Herron was quoted as saying she thought that black people had moved beyond equating nappy hair with bad hair during the 1960s. Clearly, they had not.

On one level, Bristol's concerns are rooted in the popular black mantra: it's a black thing, you wouldn't understand. On another level, his questions demonstrate the apprehension many black

people feel in airing intraracial issues, otherwise known as "dirty
laundry" to those outside black communities. This was a point re-
layed to me by one of the black women I interviewed for *Hair
Matters*. "What is the significance of your book? What are you
trying to prove?" Patricia's question during an evening focus-
group session with four black women in their early twenties
echoed in my head as I wrote down postinterview notes later that
night. Her question forced me to begin thinking about how I
would engage that question in the book. I certainly wasn't trying
to prove that hair matters to all African American women in the
same ways. I did, however, want to produce a book that illustrates
why hair matters to African American women. But Patricia ap-
parently believed that by highlighting the tensions that surround
hair among African Americans, I was adding to the controversy.
Why, she seemed to be asking, add fuel to the fire, given that the
book will be read not only by black women, but by others as
well?

If the events that unfolded at P.S. 75 tell us anything, they make
it evident that something greater is at stake than concerns about
airing dirty laundry for mainstream consumption. Black life and
culture are consumed on many different levels in U.S. society on
a daily basis, as the national coverage of the P.S. 75 incident
demonstrates. Black people simply can't police mainstream consumption of black culture. My main intent after reading article
after article about the meetings and discussions that ensued after
Ms. Sherman left P.S. 75 was in how the kids involved are dealing
with this matter. Specifically, do the black and Hispanic kids, regardless of their own hair texture, understand the historical context of "nappy" and its relationship to Herron's subversion of that
history? Do they interpret Herron's story and their teacher's rep-
rimand for reading it as meaning that a story that celebrates
nappy hair is "wrong" and therefore nappy hair is "bad"? These
questions point to a larger concern: how do black people's perceptions of blackness relate to how race is constructed in U.S. society and to racism?

The research presented in the following pages is not about hair
per se. *Hair Matters* illustrates how hair shapes black women's
ideas about race, gender, class, sexuality, images of beauty, and
power. The events surrounding P.S. 75 demonstrate the tensions

that surface when social and cultural ideas are transmitted through bodies. As black women and girls explain throughout this book, hair is a means by which one can understand broader cultural issues. If cultural theorists want to understand how black women and girls view their worlds, it is essential to understand why hair matters to them. As Wixie, a forty-five-year old physician, stated at the beginning of a focus-group session for *Hair Matters:* "There's always a question of race, money, and sex. But I think for black women, it's race, money, sex, and hair. It transcends a cosmetic [or esthetic] issue because it is at the base historically, culturally, and socially."

Missing from discussions about black women and hair was a book focusing on how black women link hair to broader social and cultural ideas, and this book aims to fill the gap. After all, shouldn't black women address questions of the relationship, if any, between, say, hairstyling practices and self-esteem? This topic is one of the many issues simmering in academic and popular debates that we will examine in *Hair Matters.* The book is part of a general body of scholarship that investigates the social and cultural import of hair. To understand how *Hair Matters* is positioned within and outside of previous theorizing about hair, we must assess how scholars have come to associate the relationship between hair and broader cultural and social forces.

Situating Hair in Academia

Over the past century, hair has received considerable attention in academic circles among psychoanalysts, sociologists, and anthropologists. In general, the earlier debates focused on the symbolic meanings of hair, but in time specific themes reacting to previous hair theorizing emerged. For example, studies using psychoanalytical theory as a basis for discussing the general topic of hair began with Freud (1922) in the widely cited essay "Medusa's Hair." Freud argues that the decapitated head of Medusa symbolizes castration. Medusa's mouth and hair, according to Freud, symbolize the female genitals and therefore create castration anxiety in males. Another psychoanalyst,

Charles Berg, went a step farther than Freud in *The Unconscious*
Significance of Hair (1951), in which he cited ethnographic evidence when he concluded that castration anxiety was at the root of all hair practices, regardless of gender or cultural particularities. Whereas Freud and Berg theorized about the unconscious meanings of hair, anthropologist Edmund Leach challenged this psychoanalytic tradition in the essay "Magical Hair" (1958) by arguing that symbols have public origins. As such, symbols have little, if any, meaning within the unconscious. In "Social Hair" (1972), C. R. Hallpike criticizes Leach for going overboard with psychoanalytic theory. He argues that instead of being a badge of desire, hair represents social control. For example, soldiers and prisoners wear short hair. On the other hand, long-haired hippies and women exist on the fringes of the social structure. In "Hair, Sex, and Dirt" (1974), P. Hershman presents an ethnography that focuses on hair symbolism within Hindu and Sikh Punjabi cultures and argues that hair scholarship must take into account culturally specific realities.

However, it was Leach's research that stimulated several responses within the anthropological community. For example, in *Medusa's Hair: An Essay on Personal Symbols and Religious Experience*, Gananath Obeyesekere (1981) argues that Leach should have given more credence to psychoanalysis. In a discussion on public and private symbols, using ethnographic evidence, Obeyesekere argues that private symbols originate within the unconscious, but these symbols may or may not develop public significance.

Hair theorists began to consider other issues besides hair symbolism as well. In *Hair: Sex, Society, and Symbolism*, Wendy Cooper (1971) discusses both biological and social issues surrounding hair. She contends that hair is an "easily controlled variable that can denote status, set fashion, or serve as a badge" (p. 7). As a result, hair has emerged as socially and culturally significant. Cooper also argues that skin and hair, respectively, are the two most important physical attributes for racial classification. For example, she notes that hair not only varies in terms of type and texture among different races but also within race categories. Cooper offers some insight on the issue of hair and gender as well. Similar to arguments in the anthropological literature,

Cooper engages the pervasiveness of the historical fascination with hair as a gauge of female attractiveness.

In recent debates among anthropologists, hair symbolism continues to be important, but different arguments are being presented. In "Hairdos and Don'ts: Hair Symbolism and Sexual History in Samoa" (1994), Jeannette Mageo argues that Leach's point concerning the potency of body symbols is much more detailed because "while body symbols like hair may be psycho-genetic, when they become a part of public culture they lose unconscious motivational significance for those who employ them in public social life" (p. 20). Whereas Obeyesekere (1981) argues, based on his ethnographic data from interviews with female ascetics in India, that public symbols often gain unconscious meaning due to a traumatic experience in the life of an individual, Mageo points out that "[i]t seems more likely that public symbols acquire private significance for all of us simply because public social life affects us personally: what has personal significance is at least in part a product of how we are regarded and treated by others" (p. 21).

In *Off with Her Head! The Denial of Women's Identity in Myth, Religion, and Culture,* edited by Eilberg-Schwartz and Doniger (1995), theorists focus on the female head as a site of social, cultural, and religious meanings. Howard Eilberg-Schwartz argues that gendered meanings of hair have been absent in earlier debates about hair symbolism. In "Shaven Heads and Loose Hair: Buddhist Attitudes toward Hair and Sexuality," Karen Lang (Eilberg-Schwartz and Doniger 1995) challenges Berg's reductionist argument that generalizes hair symbolism to both women and men and all cultures. She notes that the meanings of hair mean different things for women, for men, and in different cultural contexts. In "Untangling the Meaning of Hair in Turkish Society," Carol Delaney (Eilberg-Schwartz and Doniger 1995) makes an argument similar to Lang's, substantiating her claims through ethnographic research in Turkey. Delaney argues that in some instances, hair symbolism can be applied cross-culturally. Nevertheless, hair meanings, in most cases, are specific to individual cultures. Indeed, discussions about the meanings of hair in relationship to blacks point to the importance of culturally specific analyses.

The scholarship on blacks and hair covers topics similar to those presented above, as well as different ones. In the following discussions, scholars focus on hair symbolism, but they do not present their arguments through ethnographic studies, nor do they focus their analyses on sexual symbolism and public and private symbols. Although subconscious understandings of hair do emerge, these discussions are never completely within the realm of the subconscious as argued by general hair theorists such as Freud (1922) and Berg (1951). Furthermore, scholars focusing on blacks and hair emphasize the importance of hair among blacks in relationship to Africa, constructions of race, enslavement, skin color, self-esteem, ritual, esthetics, appropriate grooming practices, images of beauty, politics, identity, and the intersection of race and gender.

To begin, in *400 Years without a Comb,* Willie Morrow (1973) chronicles the history of black hairstyling practices. He uses Africa as a point of departure, and discusses the significance of hair and hair grooming practices among people of African descent for the last four hundred years. Morrow argues that skin color and "curly or kinky hair" (p. 15) are so intertwined that it is hard to separate the two when examining the forces that shape black people's lives. He also notes that in many African societies, hairstyles are symbolic of age, occupation, clan, and status.[1] In a more general sense, Morrow argues that "[h]air is the basic, natural symbol of the things people want to be . . . and it's social-cultural significance should not be underestimated" (p. 17). Morrow further argues that once Africans were enslaved, their skin color could be "tolerated by masters," but not their hair. In fact, the curl of the hair was used to justify the subordination of Africans, which initiated the tension between hair and people of African descent in the New World. As a result, Morrow argues, the comb[2] and other grooming utensils were left behind as symbols that denoted culture, tribe affiliation,[3] and adornment. Whereas curly and kinky hair was glorified in West African societies, it became a symbol of inferiority once enslaved Africans reached American shores. Thus the pride and elegance that once symbolized curly and kinky hair immediately became a badge of racial inferiority.

Like Morrow, Orlando Patterson (1982) makes a distinction between hair and race as markers of a disempowerment system during the antebellum period. In *Slavery and Social Death: A Comparative Study,* he discusses the historical significance of hair in his analysis of the relationship between power and enslavement. In further agreement with Morrow, Patterson argues that hair, not skin color, became the more potent mark that symbolized servitude during the enslavement period in North America and the Caribbean. He notes, "Hair type rapidly became the real symbolic badge of slavery, although like many powerful symbols it was disguised, in this case by the linguistic device using the term 'black,' which nominally threw the emphasis to color" (p. 61).

In the essay "Black Hair/Style Politics," Kobena Mercer (1990) argues that hair is second only to skin color as a racial signifier. In addition, unlike Morrow and Patterson, he argues that skin color and hair among blacks are *racial signifiers*. He continues by discussing the intersection of issues involving esthetics, societal norms, internalized notions of superiority/inferiority, history, adornment, politics, and race and racism and their impact on black hair styling practices. Mercer criticizes psychological interpretations[4] of hairstyling practices that are often espoused by nationalists in the form of discussions about self-hatred. Unlike assimilationists and nationalists, he argues that these practices should be read as cultural artifacts or adornment rituals.

By the early part of the twentieth century, African Americans began associating hairstyles with their ability to achieve economic success in a segregated society. In "Black Hairstyles: Cultural and Socio-political Implications," Bruce Tyler (1990) provides a historical map of black hairstyling trends beginning in the nineteenth century. He gives ample time to assimilationist and nationalist assessments of grooming practices, particularly concerning hairstyles. Whereas the assimilationist standpoint views hair and its relationship to appropriate grooming practices as a positive factor among African Americans, nationalists view any hairstyling choices that alter black hair as signifying self-hatred. Tyler criticizes the presumption of the self-hatred theory as argued by nationalists and scholars such as Grier and Cobbs (1968).

By the late 1960s, similar debates of hair-grooming practices and what they represent emerged within academia, specifically in relationship to black women. In their widely read text, *Black Rage,* William H. Grier and Price M. Cobbs (1968) focus on the issue of what they term "achieving womanhood" for African American women. They belong to the nationalist school of thought regarding hair alteration. The two psychiatrists argue that the process of grooming hair is not only painful for black girls, but the end result is that black female children look simply acceptable rather than beautiful. One of Grier and Cobbs's conclusions is that girls receive the message that their hair in its natural state is undesirable, otherwise they would not have to endure the pain of getting their hair straightened. The psychiatrists also discuss the differences of hair grooming processes between African American and white women. For example, even if white women endure pain while grooming their hair, the result is that their beauty is enhanced—a beauty, the authors argue, that is already celebrated even before they enter the hair salon. In black women, on the other hand, not only are their features uncelebrated, but they must also submit to the humiliating pressing comb to be deemed presentable.

More recently, Robin D. G. Kelley (1997) and Maxine Craig (1997) have considered the relationship between constructions of race and gender within the context of African American hairstyling practices. In "Nap Time: Historicizing the Afro," Kelley chronicles the emergence of the Afro prior to the late 1960s and early 1970s. Kelley argues that "[t]he Afro has partial roots in bourgeois high-fashion circles in the late 1950s and was seen by the black and white elite as a kind of new female exotica" (p. 341). Kelley's discussion not only rescues the Afro from a black power masculinist narrative, but it also illustrates the difference that gender makes in the politicization of black hair: "For black women, more so than black men, going 'natural' was not just a valorization of blackness or Africanness, but a direct rejection of a conception of female beauty that many black men themselves had upheld" (p. 348). Craig makes the same argument in "The Decline of the Conk; or, How to Read a Process" when she argues that in the 1960s "[w]hen women first started wearing natural hairstyles, they felt pulled between feminine ideals and racial pride. Unlike men who moved towards more conventional gender identities by ceasing to straighten their hair, women who wore their hair in naturals broke with dominant norms of femininity (p. 414). Craig also notes that "the dominant interpretation of African American male and female hair straightening has been that it expressed identification with a white hair aesthetic" (p. 402). In challenging nationalists and others such as Grier and Cobbs (1968), Craig argues that the self-hatred or the "desire to be white" interpretation misses the various meanings that black people assign to straightened hair. In responding to a question about the meaning of hair straightening among black women during an interview for this book, seventy-year-old Mrs. Franklin said she would say the following to those who chastise black women for straightening their hair: "I would say to them, I'm not trying to do anything to look like a white person. I'm trying to improve my looks, not taking after a white or trying to be like a white person." The scholarship on blacks and hair that focuses on gender differences in understanding hairstyling practices is similar to that within general hair theorizing scholarship (Eilberg-Schwartz and Doniger 1995). Indeed, several black female scholars have made similar claims.

Hair and Black Women: The Difference Gender Makes

Several works have been written that engage beauty culture and black women (Giddings 1984; Hill Collins 1990; Caraway 1991; Rooks 1996). Discussions by black women moved the debate about the hair of those of African descent to a focus on experience (Okazawa-Rey et al. 1986; Benton Rushing 1988; hooks 1988; Walker 1988; Hill Collins 1990; Caldwell 1991; Norsworthy 1991; Cleage 1993; Wade Gayles 1993; Davis 1994; Jones 1994; Gibson 1995; Rooks 1996). In these works the authors discuss their own experiences involving hair, intersecting with race, gender, motherhood, freedom, law, appropriation, and identity. Personal anecdotes are the foundation for most of these discussions. For example in "The Making of a Permanent Afro," Gloria Wade Gayles (1993) discusses how the Civil Rights movement influenced her decision to wear an Afro because wearing her hair relaxed[5] seemed contradictory to affirming blackness. This discussion is important given its relevance to political meanings of hair that ultimately shape perceptions about the "appropriate" picture of a nationalist. Wade Gayles theorizes about the ways in which political, cultural, and social ideas shape how hair, or more generally the body, is both displayed and interpreted. Hence, hair becomes a political statement. In recognizing the importance of experience and its relationship to understanding the forces that shape black women's lives, the work of Hill Collins (1986, 1989, 1990), Christian (1988), Caldwell (1991), and Bobo (1995) demonstrate how black women theorize about their experiences through everyday narratives and discussions. Indeed, black women's ideas about hair represent how they negotiate complex identity politics. Coming-of-age stories also detail hair that include personal reflections on "good" and "bad" hair (Gibson 1995). Like Wade-Gayles (1993), Gibson places hair with race and gender as one of the most important daily issues black women face.

In one of the most important texts focusing on black women and hair, *Hair Raising: Beauty, Culture, and African American Women,* Noliwe Rooks (1996) examines black hair-care advertisements at the turn of the century. She shows how dominant or mainstream ideologies of race and beauty forced African American women to produce and sell beauty products for an African American female market. She discusses the life of Madame C. J. Walker, who is credited with inventing the straightening or pressing comb as well as marketing several other beauty aids for African American women. Through the content analysis of advertisements, Rooks sheds light on the various meanings of hair in African American communities while using Walker's life as a backdrop to discuss how U.S. beauty culture has historically related to African American women. Accounts of early black beauty culture and the enterprising Madame Walker clarify the contemporary black women's engagement with today's beauty culture. Rooks also shares a personal anecdote to relate her experiences to broader conceptualizations of identity. She describes a moment of tension when, at age thirteen, after beginning a new school, she decided that she wanted to straighten her hair so that she could be like the other girls. However, she could find no way to explain to her mother that her desire for straight hair was not a rejection of her Africanness, something her mother wanted to celebrate. In fact, Rooks frames the tension between herself and her mother as not only within the context of hair as representing political versus personal choice, but also within the framework of one's failure as a parent to instill a healthy view of self to one's child. Rooks tried to argue that straightened hair was very much a part of African American culture, especially as presented in popular African American magazines such as *Essence* and *Ebony*. To no avail Rooks explains, "My mother said no, and for the next few days I received nonstop speeches on why my hair was fine the way it was as well as on the political implications of my even asking to change it. For her, there could be no true understanding of and pride in my ancestry if I chose to straighten my hair, and she voiced great concern regarding my self-esteem and beliefs about my identity in relation to the larger society" (1996, p. 3).

Hair and the Difference Race Makes among Women

Like the early anthropological writings that don't consider the difference that culture and gender make in understandings about hair, early feminist discussions about the relationship between femininity and hair focus on hair as an indelible marker of femininity. For example, Susan Brownmiller (1984) conflates the meanings of hair by reducing the interpretation of "good" and "bad" hair to mean the same for both black and white women. For example, she assumes that among black women, "bad" hair is "limp" and "stringy." Although Brownmiller uses fiction by Toni Morrison and poetry by Ntozake Shange as a platform to discuss "good" and "bad" hair, her definitions and interpretations miss what these terms mean when black women writers use them. Instead of attempting to understand these meanings in a more nuanced fashion, Brownmiller collapses the terms into meanings that seem, as she notes, to "speak for themselves." However these meanings don't speak for themselves across racial lines, nor cultural ones, particularly when comparing white and black women.

For example, "bad" hair within black communities is not the same as "having a bad hair day." "Bad" hair speaks to the texture of tightly coiled black hair that is juxtaposed with straighter hair, otherwise known as "good" hair. Instead of understanding "bad" and "good" within different racial and cultural contexts, Brownmiller erases the differences between black and white women.[6] Her analysis demonstrates why these types of comparisons are problematic and how they disclaim the cultural significance of hair for black women by treating the issue as if it were merely a *women's* issue.

In a more general sense, earlier feminist treatments about the female body center on its objectification (de Beauvoir 1961). In recent years, however, feminist scholars have viewed the female body as a foundation not only for discussing gender and power, but as being both biologically and socially constructed (Goldstein 1991; Bordo 1989, 1993; Butler 1993). In fact, some feminist scholars argue that the poststructuralist move to deconstruct the body actually renders the physical matter of the body as invisible.[7] Unlike Brownmiller (1984), Bordo (1993) discusses the difference that *difference* makes when understanding how and why hair matters among women. In a discussion about the preoccupation with altering the body[8] and general ideas about beauty and femininity for all women, Bordo addresses the contextual meanings of hair among black women vis-à-vis white women (ibid., pp. 254–256). Similar to other hair theorists, Bordo demonstrates why culturally specific analyses of hair shed light on different meanings of hair among different groups, especially different groups of women.

Hair Matters shares the ethnographic basis of sociological and anthropological hair studies in its investigation of why hair matters among black women. As more recent hair theorists argue, cultural as well as gender differences must be considered when assessing why hair matters. Though theorizing among scholars investigating the significance of hair among blacks makes a similar assessment, few scholars have explicitly demonstrated why gender matters in hair issues among U.S. blacks (Craig 1997; Kelley 1997).

In addition, though *Hair Matters* specifically focuses on how hair shapes black women's ideas about everything from racial identity to constructions of femininity, black hair in general has

not escaped political readings about how blacks construct identities, as well as how whites construct identities about blacks by
reading the biological (hair) through a sociopolitical lens. Academic discussions about black hair only reveal part of the story, particularly given how black hair and hairstyling practices have
been read and continue to be read in a late-twentieth-century U.S.
context. Within popular discussions, tensions regarding the subject emerge that are both obvious and subtle.

Situating Black Hair in Political and Popular Culture

Black hair is certainly not simply an academic matter. The debates that scholars engage in are clearly indicative of real-world
tensions, as the literature on blacks and hair and the P.S. 75 in-
cident hitting the news scene overnight demonstrate. Within
one month, the *Nappy Hair* story was covered in the *New York
Times* at least four times and was picked up by the Associated
Press as well. It was highlighted in the *Washington Post,
Newsweek, Publishers Weekly,* the *Boston Globe, New York Daily
News, New York Post,* the *Kansas City Star, Education Week,
Tabloid,* and *JINN Magazine* (Pacific News Service). NBC's *The
Today Show,* ABC News, Fox News, and *The Montel Williams
Show* also covered the controversy. In connection with the
story, Carolivia Herron was slated to appear on *NBC Nightly
News,* ABC's *World News Tonight,* and Johnnie Cochran's *Court
TV.* The *Nappy Hair* controversy made evident to the world
what black people already know: black hair can lead to intrara-
cial and interracial tensions.

This controversy, then, was hardly the first of its kind in the
popular culture. Spike Lee films such as *School Daze* and *Jungle
Fever,* as well as the prime-time television shows *New York Un-
dercover* and *The Practice* have engaged the politically charged
issue of black women's hair. Rap artists have added to the discussion as well. Hip-hop giant Lauryn Hill, her Fugees crew, and the
Lost Boyz have laced particular songs with explicit references to
nappy hair.[9] But preceding the attention given to black hair on

prime time and in popular music in the 1990s, than was the emergence of the Afro almost three decades ago.

Though today the Afro has less political meaning, in the late 1960s it was associated with both a movement and a black woman. The movement was black power and the black woman was (and still is, even without her late 1960s, early 1970s Afro) Angela Davis. Davis has discussed her ambivalence about being reduced to a hair-do (Davis 1994), but her association with the Afro had more subtle implications. In discussing the power of her image on the FBI's "wanted" posters in 1970, Davis observes:

> While the most obvious evidence of their evidence of their power was the part they played in structuring people's opinion about me as a "fugitive" and a political prisoner, their broader and more subtle effect was the way they served as generic images of Black women who wore their hair "natural." From the constant stream of stories I have heard over the last twenty-four years (and continue to hear), I infer that hundreds, perhaps even thousands, of Afro-wearing Black women were accosted, harassed, and arrested by police, FBI, and immigration agents during the two months I spent underground. One woman, who told me that she hoped she could serve as a "decoy" because of her light skin and big natural, was obviously conscious of the way the photographs constructed generic representations of young Black women. Consequently, the photographs identified vast numbers of my Black female contemporaries who wore naturals (whether light- or dark-skinned) as targets of repression. This is the hidden historical content that lurks behind the continued association of my name with the Afro. (Ibid., p. 42)

During an interview for *Hair Matters*, Taylor, a forty-eight year old accountant, reminisced about her desire to wear an "Angela Davis Afro" during the early 1970s. Similar to Davis, who believed that law enforcement officers used her Afro as a reason to detain and harass black women, Taylor explained that it was her Afro and *assumed* gender that led to her detention during the early 1970s:

When Afros came out, I wanted to wear an Afro. So I did everything and I finally got me a great big huge Angela Davis Afro. Whenever I would wear my Afro I'd get pulled over by the police because I drove a very sleek car and they always thought from the back of the head that I had to be male a lot of times because we [Black women and Black men] all wore the same hairstyle.

Taylor's understanding of why she was detained by police officers was based on both her Afro and mistaken-gender identity. Whereas Taylor presented an image of the Afro-wearing militant being male, as supported by the general perception of the black militant at the time, Davis describes how race and gender merged to stigmatize and repress black women, a point that would surface almost twenty years later when black women's hair was at the center of legal battles.

In the late 1980s, black female employees went to court to challenge a policy by Hyatt Hotels and American Airlines against wearing braids.[10] These companies couched their policy in terms that related to "appropriate" grooming practices, which they argued braids violated. In November 1996, another hair controversy hit a suburban middle school in Chicago. The *Atlanta Journal/Atlanta Constitution* ran a story that highlighted a ban on hairstyles, along with certain clothes and jewelry that school officials defined as "gang-related paraphernalia." Hairstyles such as cornrows, dreadlocks, braids, and ponytails for boys would lead to suspension; hairstyles with zigzag parts for girls were disallowed. As with Hyatt Hotels and American Airlines, critics argued that the school's policy appeared to restrict African Americans.

Prior to the *Nappy Hair* controversy, the weekly ABC news show *20/20* aired a segment that examined the tensions that many black professional women face when it comes to hair. Oprah Winfrey dedicated an entire show to the "black hair question." As the *Los Angeles Times* reported in an article that examined the rise in natural hairstyles among black women (and men), the *20/20* episode illustrated how "[o]ne woman was terminated because management saw her hairstyle as 'extreme,' and another woman was written up because her braids were deemed 'too ethnic'" (George 1998).

In the late 1990s, descriptions of budding tennis prodigy Venus Williams and basketball sensation Allen Iverson often included references to their hairstyles, braided and in rows, respectively. The coded racial language of sportscasters' coverage of Williams's tennis matches or Iverson's basketball games is indicative of the fascination and discomfort that white mainstream U.S. society continues to feel regarding African Americans in general, and particular black hairstyles and what they signify, whether real or imagined. Like the Afro, Williams's beaded braids and Iverson's cornrows are exotic to some and threatening to others because they display a black esthetic that is linked to an authentic or radical blackness in the imagination of many whites. As Aria stated in an interview for *Hair Matters*, "I don't think that if you go on an interview and have dreads down your back that you may get as far as someone who comes in there with a nice cut, you know, clean-cut kind of hairdo. That's part of the social construction, the society we're living in, that certain esthetics are more acceptable than other esthetics." In a *Sports Illustrated* article focusing on basketball star Iverson, ample discussion was given to his cornrows by the reporter: "Iverson sports the rows because he knows they make him different from the wack suits in Philly who pay $54 a ticket to watch him, knows they make him different from the writers who rip him. It's his I.D. in the Hip Hop Nation, as he calls it. Ask Spike Lee what keeps America from embracing one of the most entertaining young players in the NBA and Lee doesn't hesitate: 'The braids'" (Reilly 1998, p. 86). Recently, Latrell Sprewell's cornrows made the spotlight. Replying to a question during an interview with a *New York Times* reporter about his hair's giving him the image of a thug, Sprewell stated: "I just like to be different. . . . I know some people might be threatened by the hair-*style,* but I like not being like everybody else" (Berkow 1999, D1). In other words, black hair and hairstyling practices can never escape political readings. The motivation of the person sporting the hairdo is irrelevant. Black hair and hairstyling practices are politicized. Just ask Angela Davis.

Though black (female) scholars have provided important discussions that link hair and personal identity, an empirically based book has been absent in the literature. Therefore, I asked black girls and women their thoughts about hair to gain an even greater understanding of how hair meanings represent broader articulations about beauty, power, and black women's consciousness. By consciousness, I mean a consciousness that represents difference and the multiple realities that black women face. A social and political history and reality exist that constitute what it means to be black and female in a racist and sexist society. Whether these ideas are embedded in the historical constructions of Mammy, Sapphire, and Jezebel (Giddings 1984; Roberts 1997; St. Jean and Feagin 1998), being black has a political and social context in U.S. society, particularly being a black woman. Although analyses of what constitutes "blackness" provide an important challenge to reductionist constructions of black identity, they do harm when they are applied to historical and political understandings of what it means to be black in U.S. society now and in the past. Although a black women's consciousness is not essentialist in assuming that all black women are alike, we know that as a group, black women have a particular historical and political reality in the United States. The chapters presented in *Hair Matters* not only show how black women as individuals understand their lives, but how individual black women understand how black women as a group experience beauty culture in American society.

Points of Departure

Ethnographic at heart, *Hair Matters* presents data collected from interviews with sixty-one black girls and women, consisting of forty-three individual interviews and five focus-group sessions. The interviews were conducted during the Fall of 1996 and early winter 1997.[11] Chapter 1 lays the foundation for the text by posing this fundamental question: Why does hair matter among African American women? The first chapter illustrates how hair shapes black women's ideas about race, gender, and beauty culture. Chapter 2 addresses the self-hatred theory of hair alteration among black women. The girls and women with whom I spoke made comments that support and challenge the self-hatred theory in insightful ways. The first two sections of chapter 3 discuss the relationship between hair, power, and choice. I asked the girls and women two questions: (1) Is hair associated with power in any way? and (2) Do African American women have a choice or voice (i.e., one that is independent of societal norms or beliefs) about the way they wear their hair? Their answers make it evident that black girls and women feel strongly about questions relating to identity. The final section of chapter 3 investigates the relationship between hair and femininity. Within this discussion, the relationship between hair and sexuality surfaced as well, thereby providing a greater understanding of how black women develop ideas about womanhood. Chapter 4 presents discussions from five focus groups comprised of friends. The five individual groups consisted of teens, women in their early twenties, graduate students, physicians, and low-income women. I also provide a brief description of each focus group's setting. Chapter 5 addresses black hairstyling practices in the 1990s. The conclusion sums up some of my major findings and provides suggestions for further research.

Those interested in how I went about collecting data for *Hair Matters* should read the appendixes first, which also present important information and terms that some readers may find useful. Appendix I presents a discussion of methods and methodology. I not only discuss how I recruited girls and women to be interviewed, but methodological issues and questions that emerged as I collected data. Readers interested in how I positioned myself as a black woman conducting research on black women and what expectations I had will find this discussion worth reading. Appendix II presents three tables of black hair and hairstyling terms. Tables 1 and 2 present the terms I used and operationally defined in grouping the girls and women based on hair types/texture and hairstyles, and table 3 is a glossary of popular black hair and hairstyling terms. Appendix III provides a list of the interviewees and demographic data. Although three of the women requested that I use their real names,[12] all other names, excluding mine, have been changed in the transcribed responses that serve as the backdrop for the text.

Hair Matters explains why the P.S. 75 incident escalated the way it did—why a seemingly innocent book about a black girl's nappy hair could cause so much controversy. When Ruth Sherman shared *Nappy Hair* with her students, she probably did not anticipate the firestorm that would ensue. Cathy Wright's statement that Herron's book did not make her or her daughter feel good about being black and female showed that black women in particular, and black people in general, continue to embrace standards of beauty that exist both within and outside of black communities. *Nappy Hair* challenges the very things that so many blacks have been socialized to reject: black physical characteristics that do not meet the standard of what is considered beautiful.

How, then, do black women reinforce and challenge constructions of beauty in their communities and in mainstream society? Why do some women enforce such ideas while others reject them? Why do some women reinforce these ideas as they attempt to actually subvert them? Why were some black Brooklyn residents so outraged by a children's book that affirms the physical characteristics of countless black girls? It doesn't matter whether we agree or disagree with Cathy Wright's assessment of Herron's book; what matters is our ability to understand why a book that glorifies physical characteristics of black girls would receive a reply of "no thanks" among so many blacks. These issues, as well as others, are addressed in this book as the girls and women explain why hair matters. Wright is not alone in her view, but in the pages that follow, her perspective is placed within a context that not only illustrates how her view is reinforced, but is challenged as well.

chapter 1

Why Hair Matters
Getting to the Roots

I think it's an issue because it doesn't function in a vacuum. Its like connected to the larger issue of race and beauty.

> **Stacy**
> 26 years, natural hairstyle

Yes hair is important, particularly for black women. I think more so than any other woman. And it's because we learn at a very early age whether we have good or bad hair, and that automatically places us in two [camps].

> **Sheila**
> 36 years, dreadlocks

I think for women, in general [it's a big issue]. I like to fix my own hair in different types of styles. And I think it does something for me as far as being creative, 'cause hair can say a lot about you as a person, something about your character.

> **Barbara**
> 49 years, relaxed hairstyle

No I don't [think it's a big issue]. The reason I don't is because I know how to press mine, my mother used to press mine, and I watched her press my sister's hair and it's not hard to do.

> **Bobbie**
> 70 years, pressing comb style

Black women share a collective consciousness about hair, though it is articulated in a variety of ways. The first question I asked the girls and women is how and why hair matters. Given the many personal reflective writings by black women about their hair, I wanted the girls and women to explain if hair is important to them, too, or if the attention it gets is a lot of hype. The responses varied, but most of the women agreed that hair matters in some way to them in particular or to black women in general. It immediately became apparent to me that some of the women were having a dialogue, if not a debate, across interviews.

Social, Cultural, and Personal Contexts of Hair

Most of the girls and women in the individual interviews discussed the social, cultural, and personal reasons of why hair matters. Their thoughts demonstrate the importance of racial and gender ideologies and how they shape what black women think about beauty culture. That is, their comments detail how constructions of beauty intersect along the lines of race and gender for black women and how ideas about beauty often relate to devaluing, as opposed to embracing, tightly coiled black hair. Furthermore, the idea also emerges that black women go through a socialization process in which hair is central. For example, Kaliph, who wears her hair relaxed, and Indigo, who wears dreadlocks, discussed socialization in addition to their ideas about gender and race.

KALIPH: I think hair is a big deal for a number of reasons. Hair in general for women is a big deal because there's the whole mythology of it being our crown and glory kind of thing, and I think that it becomes even more complex when you break it down according to ethnicity. So I think compounded to us being women there's the whole thing of being black women and the devaluation of our natural hair texture. . . . So therefore you have this whole movement industry of hair-care products in general, but also in terms of black women for changing the very nature of our hair, the natural state of our hair. So I think it's a big deal for black women because we are not taught, socialized, to like our natural hair.

INDIGO: I think hair has always been a big issue for black women just because of societal values in terms of media and images that we're inundated with. And for myself, growing up in Jamaica which was a predominantly black country, I was inundated with Western images of beauty and hair. Magazines, TV commercials, TV shows [which showed] that basically the standard of beauty was always blonde and straight. And so I think for black women in a society in which our hair is unique and different from other cultures' texture, we stand out as a result of that and we've been conditioned from children to believe that there's something wrong with our hair texture in its nappy state.

Kaliph and Indigo framed their discussions within a broader context—that hair shapes black women's ideas about race, gender, and beauty. Although it is of some importance for all women, hair matters in different ways for black women, a point that Bordo (1993) makes:

When we look at the pursuit of beauty as a normalizing discipline, it becomes clear that not all body transformations are the same. The general tyranny of fashion—perpetual, elusive, and instructing the female body in a pedagogy of personal inadequacy and lack—is a powerful discipline for the normalization of *all* women in this culture. But even as we are all normalized to the requirements of appropriate feminine insecurity and preoccupation with appearance, more specific requirements emerge in different cultural and historical contexts, and for different groups. When Bo Derek put her hair in cornrows, she was engaging in normalizing feminine practice. But when Oprah admitted on her show that all her life she has desperately longed to have "hair that swings from side to side" when she shakes her head, she revealed the power of racial as well as gender normalization, normalization not only to "femininity," but to the Caucasian standards of beauty that still dominate on television, in movies, in popular magazines. (pp. 254–256)

Kaliph and Indigo also provided insight into the devaluation of black hair in its natural state. Hair becomes a marker of difference that black women recognize at an early age,[1] particularly given media representations of what constitutes beauty. Further, the importance of a children's book like *Nappy Hair* that provides a positive picture of tightly coiled hair for black girls can never be overstated given prevailing images of blackness and whiteness. It's just not hair, but the texture, the curl of black hair that causes tensions. However, it is the texture in relationship to what black women see in the media and in societal representations of what is considered beautiful.

Although "natural" relates to ideas about purity as well as being an act or state that is "normal," it takes on different meanings when it is cast against straight and straightened hair. The altered nature of relaxed or permed hair is seen as "natural," whereas natural or unaltered hair is defined as "unnatural." That is, the ways in which black women are barraged with representations of beauty that are in opposition to natural, tightly coiled black hair often result in an internalization of images of beauty that in effect reject natural hair as "natural."

Omega is fifteen years old and wears her hair natural and straight. She reiterated Kaliph's and Indigo's statements above, as well as Bordo's.

OMEGA: I think like society molds you to be like, to think a certain way. It's like, you know, everything you see on TV, hear on the radio. You never really [see], they don't make [it] out to be like kinky hair is pretty, is beautiful. Because, you know, it's already in that [kinky] state. It's always like when you have blonde hair, you know, [it's] always going to be like what people think as beautiful or pretty [or] the thing to do. And having kinky hair or having nappy hair is just never one of them.

What Omega, Kaliph, and Indigo confirm are the tensions that were at the heart of the P.S. 75 incident. Nappy hair is not celebrated in a society that privileges straight (blonde) hair, and, by extension, white skin. Common in these statements is the point that the physical state of black hair takes on social meaning. Isha, however, who wears dreadlocks, addressed the issue of why hair matters differently. She discussed the social construction of hair and the internalization of beauty standards, but to her hair occupies both a physical and a metaphysical space.

ISHA: I think it just depends. I think that hair, depending on your hair, it can be a big issue. Like if your hair is catchin' energy and catchin' vibe and is alive, then it's going to be an issue because it's part of something. But it's not what it is all about, either. I think black women make it a big issue just based upon the amount of energy we put on it, but also I think certain times it is like a big deal but it's also just hair, too. Like it protects your crown, it serves a purpose and you can't get too much into it 'cause it's physical, but if it's alive and its catchin' vibe then its gon' be alive, you know what I'm saying. I think it is a big issue for blacks, I mean we make it a big issue. . . . Just because of beauty and 'cause society and low self-esteem and all that and the way we're portrayed and the way we think about ourselves. There's a bunch of little attacks that are made on black women when it comes to just our own self-spiritual wealth . . . they make all these attacks and one of them is beauty and we put so much stock into beauty. [Hair is] just a part of [your] being.

For Isha, hair matters in the sense that it is, by nature, physical, tangible. Nevertheless, hair also exists within a metaphysical and existential state that speaks to who we are as human or social beings. Because hair is attached to physical *and* social bodies, it is given meaning or "energy" because of its very relationship to the self. Hair matters because it is a part of our being, of our very existence that has meaning on the level of ideas and materiality.

Although Isha understands how hair is related to constructions of beauty that help to shape the perceptions that black women have of themselves, she nevertheless refuses to see hair as *just* a construction. Isha discusses the materiality of hair similar to Butler's (1993) argument that both the discursive nature and the materiality of the body must be retained in feminist scholarship. It is through Isha's comments that Butler's theory finds meaning: Isha not only reflects on a concern that Butler describes as doing away with the physical body in feminist theory, but she notes that there are "little attacks" on black women. In saying this, Isha shows that the black female body is attacked both materially[2] and discursively.[3]

Why Hair Matters

RENNER LEARNING RESOURCE CENTER
ELGIN COMMUNITY COLLEGE
LIGIN ILLINOIS 60123

Isha points out that although hair is a big deal, it doesn't have to be because it really is only physical matter. But she also realizes that hair is a physical manifestation of our being that becomes loaded with social and cultural meanings. Still, there seems to be a sense in Isha's comments that blacks, and black women in particular, have some "responsibility" in shaping meanings of hair because "we make it a big issue." This was the same position that some blacks took after Cathy Wright and others protested the use of *Nappy Hair* in the classroom at P.S. 75 (Nelson 1998).

Isha's comments also illustrate the cultural and social contexts of hair that go beyond its physical nature. This point serves as a metaphor for placing hair within debates about social constructions of the body and how such constructions take on meanings that challenge the mere physical or biological existence of hair. The argument that the body is a text in which a host of meanings are extracted is central to scholarship that examines social meanings of the body (de Certeau 1984; Bordo 1993; Butler 1993; Roberts 1997). Hair is another important medium by which people define others, and themselves as well. In a sense, hair emerges as a body within the social body and can reflect notions about perceptions, identity, and self-esteem.

Semple and Mariya wear their hair in natural styles, and Shannon wears a relaxed style.

SEMPLE: I think that in this society we're taught that our physical appearance says a lot about who were are, [that] we're socialized in this society. Hair really is a big issue.

MARIYA: I think it's an issue because it relates to people's identity and I still think it's a big issue because it relates to what [women] want men to think about [them] and things like that, and how we still should present ourselves.

SHANNON: Well, to me it is 'cause I feel like if my hair don't look right then I feel bad about myself. That's the only way that I can feel confident about myself, you know, as far as hair, make-up.

Whereas Semple and Mariya discuss the social dimensions of hair, Shannon uses a personal narrative that centers on grooming and looking her best. However, even in Shannon's statement the social meaning of what it means to look "right" is part of her self-esteem—it shapes her definition of the self.

Still, the above comments do not merely deal with the social meanings of hair. For example, Semple's statement about the importance of physical appearance illustrates how displaying the body is a reflection of identity. Mariya is more explicit in her analysis because she actually mentions identity, but unlike Semple, Mariya reflects on how the presentation of the body relates to an understanding about gender, specifically femininity. In fact, she relates ideas about hair to women's perceptions of what they feel men desire in a woman.

These comments actually follow on a continuum in which appearance, identity, and self-esteem intersect and overlap. When Shannon discusses how hair impacts her self-confidence, she is in effect translating Semple and Mariya's comments to a personal level that is informed by social and cultural meanings of black womanhood through an understanding about hair.

Elantra, who wears her hair in a short natural style, addressed the issues discussed above but also went beyond them. She highlighted difference as an asset for black women, something that can be celebrated and embraced.

ELANTRA: Yeah, definitely it's an issue. I guess it goes back to historical events. I think it's more of an issue now than it was in the past because in the past everyone pressed it, basically. And I think now that we have more opportunity to define ourselves, we're experimenting more with hair, and I think it's been an explosion lately with different hair types. Society dictates so many things to us, like who we are as women, who we are supposed to be as black women, especially like if you look on TV or in a film. And I think that [hair is] one of the things that we can determine about ourselves [and] we can do different things with our hair that white women can't do. So, it's sort of like an advantage that we have and a way that we can be creative and get away with it.

Elantra makes a perceptive comment about recent trends in black hairstyling practices (the focus of chapter 5). In her statement a sense of empowerment unfolds. She sees adornment practices as influencing the importance of hair, translating into an advantage for blacks. Whereas the other women discussed the devaluation of black hair in its natural tightly coiled state, Elantra, like Carolivia Herron's *Nappy Hair* that rocked P.S. 75, moved the discussion to hair and embracing positive cultural and personal definitions of self. Adornment practices are tools that black women can use in contesting mainstream notions of beauty. Although several noteworthy themes have emerged in the discussions of why hair matters, Elantra's articulation is important because it privileges *difference* in such a way that difference is good and empowering.

"Good Hair" and "Bad Hair"

The "good hair" and "bad hair" distinction is probably the most indelible construction of hair that occupies the psyche of African Americans. This is the subtext to the incidents surrounding the P.S. 75 controversy. Although the girls and women were asked a different question that addressed the subject of "good hair" and "bad hair," several of them addressed this particular dichotomy in their discussion of why hair matters to black women. Sheila's comments in the epigraph to this chapter are an excellent example of how the women articulated their feelings about "good hair" and "bad hair." After stating that "good hair" and "bad hair" puts black women in two camps, Sheila, who wears dreadlocks, added the following:

SHEILA: When you have good hair, of course you're happy about it and you feel special and more privileged than those who don't have good hair. People who don't have good hair are envious of those who do. So, yeah, it's very, very, very, very, important.

For Sheila, "good hair" has the ability to influence beliefs that go beyond the texture of one's hair. "Good hair" becomes a marker of privilege in the eyes of those who have it as well as those who don't. Both of these understandings speak to the potency of "good hair" in relationship to "bad hair." Individuals who feel special because they have "good hair" can only feel special through the existence of what has come to be known as "bad hair."

Still, Sheila attempted to subvert the term "bad hair" by calling it such as little as possible, an act that appeared to be conscious on her part. By using the term "good hair" in her discussion, Sheila challenged the idea of "bad hair" by rendering the term silent. Even though its meaning is there, she does not lend credibility to the oppressive language that some blacks feel Carolivia Herron's *Nappy Hair* supports. However, as Pearl Cleage (1993) argues, in reflecting on a childhood memory, the term "good hair" is powerful in and of itself: "Now I was only four, but I was old enough to know that 'not quite good long enough' was a polite way of saying 'not quite good enough,' as in the phrase she got that good stuff, when applied to hair. Good in this context needed no qualifiers. Good could stand alone (p. 37)."

In contrast to Sheila, Raine explicitly engaged both the ideology and terminology of "bad hair." Although she discussed "good hair" and "bad hair" in a similar way, she also explained the role of tradition and the broader societal messages on intracultural issues that maintain hierarchies among African Americans. Raine, who presses her hair with a pressing or straightening comb, supports the arguments of Morrow (1973) and Patterson (1982) about the greater importance of hair over skin color in influencing hierarchies among blacks during enslavement. Her comments also reflect the tensions displayed during the *Nappy Hair* controversy.

RAINE: Because blacks are judged on their hair. I think basically the long, straight hair people are more favorable. The shorter, kinkier, nappier [the] hair, the less favoritism is shown. I've lived that, coming through school as a young girl I was dark, but I had long hair. I was put in with the little light [skin] long-haired kids. But the ones who had the short, measly, nappy hair, no matter what they looked like, they were always last, in the back. I don't really know [why that's so]. Well, that's our race and other races do that [to us]. We do that ourselves. And I think that it's just something that's been passed on, you know, from slavery time. I think the lighter slaves and the straighter-hair slaves were the ones that were put in the big house and the other ones were out in the field. And it was just a favoritism that we took up from the white man and continued.

Using her own personal experiences and the historical observation of miscegenation and perceived privilege among some enslaved blacks, Raine argues that hair has the ability to "trump" race and skin color when assessing favoritism and privilege in inter- and intracultural settings. For example hair was more important as a marker of advantage and disadvantage than skin color on plantations. This argument is similar to Patterson's (1982) and also demonstrates how hair can denote attractiveness and privilege among blacks and how an understanding of this idea is instilled at a young age. Raine's comments situate themselves within a historical context that, she explains, has roots in mainstream society. According to Raine, favoritism based on skin color and hair is something that blacks "took up from the white man and continued," and mainstream notions of beauty have been internalized by African Americans and, as Grier and Cobbs (1968) argue, by black women in particular. Raine's comments also support Hill Collins's (1990) argument that black women's ideas about beauty are shaped through an understanding about hierarchies based on hair and skin color.

Raine also used specific terminology,[4] demonstrating Hallpike's (1972) argument that hair has social meanings. The slang term "measly"[5] for "bad hair" refers to something not fit to be touched, as well as to an entity or idea that is beneath contempt.[6] But "measly" also means "lacking" or "skimpy." Although Raine lacks light skin and "good hair," she does have long hair that facilitated her entrée into a privileged group of kids. Raine explained how hair length and skin tone can actually challenge distinctions between the texture of "good hair" and "bad hair." Elaine Brown (1992) makes a similar point in a rhyme retelling her childhood observation about hair and skin color privilege in black communities:

> *If you white, you right*
> *If you yellow, you mellow*
> *If you brown, stick around*
> *If you black, get back*
> *Way back!*

Everyone on York Street knew the truth of that rhyme. Everyone understood. Everyone had always known that dark-skinned colored girls with "bad," or kinky, hair were ugly. Everyone had always known that "high-yellow" colored girls with "good," or straight, hair were pretty. The rule was simple: The closer to white, the better. We derided girls who had short "nappy hair," or thick "liver" lips, or protruding, high behinds, or skin "so black it's blue." I did not want to get back. Despite that I was, like most girls on York Street, a few shades "too dark," I had "good" hair and white facial features. (p. 31)

Although Raine discusses hierarchies that exist between "good hair" and "bad hair," light skin and dark skin, and slaves out in the field and those in the house, her personal experiences, like Brown's, demonstrate how these ideas are not immutable: there are moments, for better or worse, when skin color determines status. Sometimes, in very complicated spaces, "bad hair" and dark skin are privileged. Yet even then, hair is the marker that denotes status or position. As Raine notes, if she would have had "measly, short, nappier" hair, she would have been less favored, thereby supporting Morrow (1973) and Patterson (1982) in their findings that hair, more than skin color, determines status. When Raine states that blacks and other races maintain a skin color system that shapes relationships among blacks, she shows that hair, as a marker, is indicative of beliefs that are based on the social construction of race in U.S. society (Omi and Winant 1984). In essence, her observations, like the arguments posed by Morrow and Patterson, cannot be reduced to hierarchies that are simply based on hair. It is what hair *means* that is key.

Senior Women and Grooming Practices

Senior black women provided a different view of why hair matters. Those born in the 1920s addressed this question within the context of grooming practices. Their comments appear to be related to age and the types of hairstyling practices they grew up with. Bobbie's comments in the epigraphs to the chapter personalize the issue by relating it to her experience and expertise in pressing her hair. Mrs. Franklin, who is seventy and also presses her hair with the pressing comb, personalized her discussion as well.

> MRS. FRANKLIN: At this present time, it's a big issue for me, but just recently it got to be a big issue 'cause I haven't had problems with my hair up until recently. It's thin, it's hard to manage, just not enough body to it. I have to roll it every night. If I don't roll it at night, then if I get up the next day and I have somewhere to go, I got to get hot curlers and different stuff and start working on it. But before, I didn't have to do that.

Although in the pages that follow, younger women do focus on grooming practices (unlike younger women such as Indigo and Kaliph), Mrs. Franklin did not discuss how the intersection of race and gender shape black women's ideas on the importance of hair. Her discussion does, however, relate to the intersection of gender and age because she is at a point in her life in which her hair is thinning, a not uncommon occurrence among women across all cultures. This concern supports the usefulness of some cross-cultural analyses that focus on gender, age, and health issues among senior women. It also shows that age matters in black women's understanding of why hair matters. It is noteworthy that Mrs. Franklin framed her response to my question in a way that if hair matters, then it must be a problem. Her reading of the question suggests that senior black women understand hair in a different context.

Both Mrs. Franklin and Bobbie were born during a time when Madame C. J. Walker's invention of the pressing comb was a recent discovery. As Bobbie noted in her comments in the epigraphs, she learned hair pressing from her mother who belonged to the first generation of black women to use the new comb, and both she and Mrs. Franklin have always pressed their hair. They have never used a relaxer or perm to straighten their hair. Despite shifts in hairstyling practices among blacks over time, Bobbie and Mrs. Franklin stayed with the pressing comb because pressing hair was familiar.

In this sense, pressing hair can be associated with tradition, and it continues to be the standard, in terms of straightening hair among black women; indeed, along with chemical relaxers, it has remained the most constant practice since the early twentieth century.[7] Women born in the 1940s and 1950s have covered the spectrum of hairstyling practices from chemical relaxers to wigs to natural styles, but not these two women in their seventies. Many of the women that I spoke to who were born in the 1940s and 1950s told me about coming of age during the mid-1960s and how the Black Power Movement shaped their hairstyling practices. By the time the "Black is Beautiful!" affirmation reached a grand scale in the late 1960s, Bobbie and Mrs. Franklin had already experienced their own coming of age. Because hair matters even to older women, we can see that one's generation or age, in part, shapes one's understanding of why hair matters.

Hair as "Insignificant"

The pervasiveness of why hair matters among black women is evident in the telling comments by those who seemed to minimize the importance of hair within the lives of black women, whether on a personal or general level. For example, although Jean, who wears her hair in a natural style, explained that maturity led her to reject the importance of hair, she still understands why it is an important issue for black women in general.

JEAN: It's no longer a big deal for me. When I was younger it was. Now I could give a damn. I can see how it can be a big deal, but it was a big deal for me when I was like in high school, early twenties, because you want to look cute for guys, and guys want the long hair, or at least it appears that way. To try to make your hair look attractive, which means trying to duplicate what you see in the media. Our hair just ain't gon' do it. So I tried and gave up. Actually, I didn't exactly give up. I developed my own beauty.

Although Jean says that she has developed her own sense of beauty, one that presumably goes against the grain of mainstream constructions of beauty, she nevertheless recognizes how images of beauty influence women's perceptions of themselves. Jean uses gender analysis to discuss how the grooming practices of women, particularly younger women, are influenced by the perception, whether real or imagined, of what men prefer. In stating that men prefer long hair, Jean explains how gender, in the form of ideas about womanhood and therefore about femininity, is constructed—long hair has become a standard that defines femininity. The media sends the message about what is deemed feminine, and therefore women make attempts to conform to a norm they believe will yield personal and social rewards.

Because Jean noted that at one time hair was a "big deal" to her, I followed up by asking if she felt hair was an issue for black women in general.

JEAN: Oh, I think incredibly, incredibly. Well, I think it's because you know you can't change your face but you can change your hair. It's cheap plastic surgery, maybe. Stick a roller in. Again, I think it goes back to that whole attractiveness thing and what is beauty.

Even within her own understanding of what is considered beautiful, Jean is nevertheless reacting to the importance of hair. It is in reaction to a mainstream construction of beauty even within her personal "post-hair-matters" perspective that Jean questions and rejects the importance of hair. Clearly, her comments signal a deconstruction of mainstream constructions of beauty, which results in embracing a very empowering sense of self. Yet such an awareness comes with age. Therefore, Jean's comments about the insignificance of hair on a personal level still shows a recognition that hair matters among black women, especially within the context of the constructions of attractiveness and beauty.

Jocelyn, an eighteen-year-old college student who wears her hair in a relaxed style, addressed the issue of why hair matters differently than Jean and other women. She felt that all the media exposure of black popular culture, and by extension, black hair,

JOCELYN: I don't think that it's that big of an issue. It's just that
people [usually] bring up the typical white girl, straight hair,
blonde hair [look]. And so now they're trying to promote
black hair. So normally when you try to promote something
you kind of overexaggerate it.

I asked Jocelyn what she thinks accounts for this overexaggera-
tion of black women's hair, and I also asked what she meant by
"overexaggerate."

JOCELYN: Just acceptance, just to get it out in the open, so that
if they overexaggerate it, obviously its gonna be [everywhere
and] everyone is gonna keep it in their minds. [I mean overexaggerate by] just promoting [black hair], you know. Just like
how they did the white people back in the day.

Instead of framing her response in a context that deals with mainstream notions of beauty, "good hair" and "bad hair," or grooming practices, Jocelyn explains that the only reason hair matters
is because recent trends in black hairstyles have made it *appear to
be an issue*. However, her comments relate to mainstream ideas.
She appears to argue that because the "white girl" look (straight
hair) has been the standard for so long, the time has come to promote black hair as a way of challenging mainstream standards regarding hair. The explosion of hip-hop, rap music, and videos and
their influence on other forms of music, television, film, fashion,
the Internet, and the advertisement industry are influencing the
exposure of black popular (youth) culture in the late twentieth
century. But mainstream (white) fascination with black culture is
not new (Rose 1994; Kelley 1997). Jocelyn knows something about
the more recent influences since she is a part of the younger generation of blacks whose culture is visible everywhere and readily
accessible to all. She seems to suggest that the larger culture now
allows for a certain level of acceptance of black hair and hairstyling practices. While the other women have suggested that
black hair, particularly when it is tightly coiled, is devalued in its

natural state and straighter hair is privileged, Jocelyn suggests that black hair, in a general sense, is being "promoted" in the same way that "white" hair was "promoted" in the past. Jocelyn's reading of the attention that black hair and hairstyles receive comes from the perspective of a late teen witnessing the appropriation of black cultural practices, such as hairstyles, music, lingo, dress, by nonblacks. Unlike Omega, for example, Jocelyn does not even engage a discussion about nappy hair, perhaps because her hair isn't nappy. As a matter of fact, although she relaxes her hair, she has what is known as "good hair." This may suggest that, along with age, hair texture also influences black women's understanding of why hair matters.

Further Articulations of Why Hair Matters

Comments by other women further demonstrate how understandings about hair transcend hair itself. Habiba, a fifty-year-old woman who wears her hair in a short-cropped natural style, discussed the significance of the tightly coiled nature of black hair in its natural state, but articulated it within a framework of the actual act of combing hair. Habiba's comments raise important debates because, although she noted that hair matters for black women because of its curl, she also argued the importance of understanding how hair is not only an issue for black women, but other groups as well. According to her, the only difference is on a material level that involves the texture of tightly coiled black hair.

HABIBA: Well, I think it's so because we have to work with it. We have a texture that we can't just leave undone. But knowing, having many good friends who are white, they have problems with their hair too, you know, they do the opposite of what we do. So we're trying to get, to do something with the curly texture and they're trying to do something with the straight texture. So I think that it's working with the curl, combing it, you know, is part of it. And also, we grow up with our mothers making a big deal of it, "now it's time to get your hair combed."

Habiba's cross-cultural point resembles Brownmiller's (1984) in that she does not differentiate between black and white women's hair "problems." Similar to Brownmiller's reading of "good hair" and "bad hair," Habiba conflates "texture" issues to mean the same for both groups of women. Indeed, all women work with their hair in some manner, but how and why black women work with it and what it means within cultural, social, and political contexts leads to cross-cultural comparisons that are weak at best.

Yet Habiba addresses intracultural understandings about hair when she ends her statement by noting how black girls grow up knowing that hair is significant. Later in the interview I asked her if hair affects other aspects of her life and, if so, did she think that was true for other black women. Although she responded by noting that time and money were significant in understanding why hair matters, she explained that "that's true for every single person." I responded by asking, "And you're saying everybody, whether black women or?" The following comment is Habiba's response to my probe and reflects her concerns with dichotomizing hair issues or even making it seem as if black women hold the "patent" on hair matters.

HABIBA: Heck no. Look in the book in the hair salon shops. I hate this balkanization, we're here, they're there. Once we learn about each other, we learn that other people have just as many concerns [then divisions will cease]. White women have tremendous concerns about having stringy hair and they spend tons of money. Asians have a very hard time getting their hair cut.

Habiba's comments still demonstrate the problem of crosscultural interpretations of hair and hairstyling practices. Instead of addressing hair as a social and cultural import that is socially, culturally, and politically loaded, Habiba stresses the commonalties such as *everybody* has to spend time and money on the upkeep of hair. In fact, she provides an analysis that in many ways relates to class realities. That is, she focuses on the fact that everybody has to spend money and time without understanding the various contexts in which the money and time are spent. Further, she explained that many white women have issues with having "stringy" hair.

But we are not here concerned with the hair grooming problems that women have in general; it is the *quality* of their concerns. Certainly white women have concerns with their hair, but their concerns do not involve the actual alteration of hair texture to the extent that it is an expression of their cultural consciousness. Within a broader context, they do not have to deal with cultural and political constructions of hair that intersect with race and gender in relationship to mainstream notions of beauty, putting a great number of black women outside of what is considered beautiful in U.S. society.[8] For black women, hair matters embody one's identity, beauty, power, and consciousness. Although Habiba's comments represent the complex and varied articulations that black women bring to discussions about hair, to stress cross-cultural commonalties with regard to hair as if they outweigh the differences lends itself to analyses such as Brownmiller's which deny racial and cultural meanings of hair. In efforts to promote utopian notions of togetherness and commonalties, these types of articulations often miss, if not delegitimize the importance of, racial difference. The same critique has been rightfully waged against class analyses, such as Marxism, that render cultural and racial differences invisible. Habiba's comments also reflect first- and second-wave feminist readings of gender that leave little or no room for differences among women based on race, class, and sexuality.

Like Habiba, some of the other women made unique comments about their perceptions of why hair matters. The following ones indicate the friction between external and internal expectations and perceptions about hair within the context of being professionally presentable. Although the women agree on the relationship between hair and professionalism, each woman addressed this relationship distinctly.

GRACE: Well, I think it's important because you want to keep your hair up and look professional for a job interview or

something like that, but I don't think all the let's stop the
perm, stop the perm, that's not all that important to me.

Grace, who wears her hair in a relaxed style, engages the issue of hairstyling practices as they relate to professional spheres. Keeping one's hair well groomed is related to looking professional, which has influenced Grace's decision to perm her hair. Although Ronnie, who wears braids with extensions, also discussed looking professional when I asked her why hair matters among black women, she used a personal platform to discuss her position.

RONNIE: Well, actually I don't know because I've heard a lot too and right now I'm undergoing a series of interviews. I'm trying to get a different [job] position. And it was suggested to me by my mother that maybe I should consider taking my braids out temporarily just until I get the position that I want. But I disagree with that because I feel that if the company doesn't want me for me, then I don't need to be there. So I go to the interviews with my braids because this is me. This isn't just a fad. I've had braids all my life and I'm not going to change for anyone so whether or not it's an issue, that's not really my concern right now. I'm just trying to do what I want to do, but I'm not going to change me.

Because I interviewed Ronnie at a time when she was attempting to secure a new job and her mother suggested she lose the braids, it is not surprising that her response reflects her adamant insistence of remaining true to herself. Unlike Grace, she challenges the perception that looking professional involves wearing one's hair straight. In contrast, Charlene's comments below reflect the tension between the social world and the professional world and how such a tension is brought to bear on hairstyling practices.

CHARLENE: I think it is a very big issue for a number of reasons. The most outstanding reason to me is career-wise, or socialization. Depending on who you want to socialize with dictates pretty much what kind of hair, what kind of style you have to wear. I'm an administrative assistant so if you want to sit at the front desk of someone's organization, it's unsaid, but

I believe that you have to have straight hair. And that's why I press my hair, although I prefer it natural. I don't have to press it here [at my job], but to go other places and do other things.

Although Charlene does not have to press her hair for her administrative position because she works for an Afrocentric company,[9] she still feels the pressure to straighten her hair because of the social pressures that arise outside of her job. In fact, she also explained that her family would be very critical if she didn't straighten her hair.

Although Charlene feels that black women have to have straight hair to get a front-office job, she did not have to straighten her hair to get hers or keep it. She prefers to wear natural hairstyles, which are not only welcomed but preferred by her employer. Charlene's thoughts and actions are guided by a socialization that points to the contradiction between hair alteration and preference. To what extent has hair alteration become a preference that is so insidious that, even in discussions about occupation and hair preference, ideas about what it means to be a black woman can surface? These issues are explored in chapter 2.

The Hair "Do's" and "Don'ts" of Black Womanhood

An activist with straightened hair was a contradiction. A lie. A joke, really.

Gloria Wade-Gayles

We knew, for example, that what's on your head is just as important as what's in it. The natural was sprouting everywhere—dark sunflowers filling a vacant field. No one could see my anger, but they could see my hair.

Marita Golden

As soon as I walk into a room and I see a black woman with relaxed hair, I immediately lose a certain amount of respect for her.

Anonymous black woman during a discussion about blacks and hair

You are considered much more feminine and much more alluring if your hair is long. The longer your hair is, the more feminine you are.

Sheila

In the Broadway play *The Colored Museum,* George C. Wolfe (1987) highlights the importance of hair among black women. In a scene entitled "The Hairpiece," Wolfe demonstrates the political, social, esthetic, and personal tensions that arise in issues surrounding hair and black women. The scene focuses on a black woman and her two styrofoam wig heads that come to life as the scene develops. One styrofoam head has long, straight hair, and the other has an Afro. The two heads, or styles as it were, engage in a debate about which style should be worn by the woman when she breaks up with her boyfriend later that day. The Afro style explains that the woman will need much attitude, which can only be fueled by the kinks of an Afro. The straight style argues that attitude is passé, having died out in 1968. This is a task for hysteria, emotion, and the only way that inner emotion can surface is when the woman has the capability to toss her tresses back in grand sweeping motions, and from side to side. A job, no doubt, for the straight look.

The provocative aspect of Wolfe's piece is that it demonstrates how hair shapes ideas about one's identity. Attitude and emotion are placed on the site of one's head, as opposed to inside one's head. In a very creative manner, Wolfe comments on how hair and hairstyles have the ability to influence our perceptions of individuals and groups. Although black women sporting Afros can be just as emotional as those with straight, shoulder-length hair, given the significance of hair in black communities and considering broader societal perceptions, we believe that the tension between the identities that each style assumes is quite real.

The politics and significance of black hair in the U.S. have a history that predates the crowning glory of the Afro during the late 1960s and early 1970s (Tyler 1990; Rooks 1996; Craig 1997; Kelley 1997; White and White 1998). In fact, the relationship between hair and society in general has been documented in many historical texts (Cooper 1971). Even the Bible discusses the strong locks of Samson. Historically, hair has held several symbolic and cultural meanings in many African societies (Morrow 1973; Sagay 1983). Although discussions about hair and people of African descent in North America have shifted over time, issues exist that have continued to reflect some of the tensions that were evident in the nineteenth and early twentieth centuries, particularly in relationship to women and definitions of beauty. For the most part, skin color and hair continue to be related to ideas about a positive notion of blackness. However, an examination that includes the gendered meanings of hair is important because racial meanings alone of hair do not take into account the complexity of the black woman's relationship to images of beauty (Craig 1997; Kelley 1997).

The historical significance of hair provides a yet broader base for understanding the social importance it carries. The social and cultural significance of black hair and hairstyling practices often centers around two main themes: politics and identity. Though Marcus Garvey and his followers and writers of the Harlem Renaissance urged blacks to cease straightening their hair and thus embrace black beauty (Craig 1997), black hair was at its height of politicization during the Black Power movement. The Afro as a symbol of black pride was ushered in on the shouts of "Black is Beautiful!" Affirming everything that is natural was just as important to the movement as black self-determination. The goal was to "move" black people to a place where they were proud of black skin and kinky or nappy hair. As a result, natural hair became a symbol of that pride, a symbol that black people were no longer "Negroes," no longer ashamed of their natural beauty. During this consciousness-raising moment emerged a right way and a wrong way to display one's political ideologies, particularly with regard to hair, as Gloria Wade-Gayles and Marita Golden's comments above reflect. Avoiding processed or straightened hair was imperative for a revolutionary or nationalist. Although both black women and men rejected straightened hair during the Black Power movement, there were different implications for black women (Craig 1997; Kelley 1997). Moreover, black women (as well as men) also rejected the belief that to get ahead in life, blacks had to partake in appropriate grooming, which included straightening their hair.

What Madame C. J. Walker attempted to offer to black women was rejected in the acceptance of the "Black is Beautiful" idea.[1] The pressing comb and chemical relaxers became oppressive because they were tools that symbolized the shame associated with black hair in its natural state. Straightening the hair became symbolic of self-hatred not only in the eyes of those in the movement, but also to some black psychiatrists. It is no surprise that in 1968, during the heyday of the Black Power movement, black psychiatrists Grier and Cobbs published a text that had ample discussion of hair alteration among black women. Although working within different theoretical traditions, black revolutionaries, nationalists, and these two psychiatrists arrived at the same conclusion: the self-hatred theory of hair alteration among black women rests on the idea that tightly coiled black hair in its natural state is undesirable or unattractive. The goal is to alter, particularly straighten, the hair through chemicals or by using the pressing or straightening comb. Proponents of the theory view hair-alteration practices among black women as indicative of a hatred of black physical features and an emulation of white physical characteristics.

Even today, this topic still holds a lot of weight. Therefore, I asked the women to address the self-hatred theory. I framed the question in the following way: There have been theories that suggest that when black women alter their hair in some form, whether by straightening it with the pressing comb or with chemicals, that they are in effect acting out some form of self-hatred. What do you think about that? The responses were quite provocative. Some demonstrate the complexity of the issue, while others show the contradictions that arise in a discussion of a highly charged topic. The discussion began by addressing the self-hatred theory, yet the women went beyond previous discussions in the literature and the self-hatred theory itself.

Approximately half of the women in the individual interviews disagreed with the self-hatred account of hair alteration. While others agreed, the level of their agreement varied because they explained how societal images and messages foster self-hatred on both a conscious and a subconscious level. Women with natural hairstyles were more likely to agree with the self-hatred theory, whereas those with altered hair were more likely to disagree. This demonstrates the generally divided perspectives that black women hold about hair alteration and how hairstyling practices may influence one's perspective on hair alteration.

Hair Alteration as Self-Hatred

Women who discussed hair alteration as self-hatred did not see the issue as precisely self-hatred, but they explained the conditions under which self-hatred is nurtured. Four of the women saw hair alteration as self-hatred, and two discussed how image, time, and energy influence hair alteration. All of these women wear their hair natural, which may contribute to their seeing hair alteration as a cultivation of self-hatred. Nia, who wears her hair in a natural short-cropped style discussed the subconscious effect of hair alteration on the self.

NIA: I tend to agree with that theory. I think that a lot of women, most women, will probably deny that. But I'm in the field of psychology and I don't think that necessarily means that that's not what's operating. I think that we've been, our oppression has been so well done. It's been so complete that we don't even know when we're acting against ourselves. And we don't even see that our own values in terms of beauty are very skewed. The contact lenses, lighter eyes. Not just the straight hair, but the longer the better. I mean, it seems pretty clear to me, and I think it is self-hatred whether it is known or not known.

Nia framed her response by explaining how the oppression of people of African descent in this country has been on such a grand scale that they have internalized the oppressor's mentality (Memmi 1965). Nia's background in psychology informs her position, but her Afrocentric perspective guides it as well.[2] Therefore, her educational background and personal and political philosophies (which are tied to her hairstyling choices) help to shape her view that hair alteration is a form of self-hatred.

Sheila wears dreadlocks and echoed Nia's words, but she put a spin on her position by placing natural characteristics within a discussion of an authentic self and how the self should not be altered except in extreme cases.

SHEILA: I think that's true, but I also think that it is so firmly ingrained in our culture, and it's so insidious, I guess. It's so subtle, that it's very hard to be aware of it and that's why for so many people it doesn't seem that way. And people will argue, well no I don't hate myself, I just like my hair this way. But really, it's just become such an automatic part of who we are that we don't think of it as self-hatred. But to me any time you can't accept yourself exactly the way God made you, that's a form of self-hate. Not just about hair but anything, you know. I mean unless it really interferes with your daily living. I mean obviously if your teeth are so crooked that it's affecting the way you eat and sleep and all that, then you should get them fixed, you know, straighten them out. But

The Hair "Do's" and "Don'ts" of Black Womanhood

when it comes to hair, if you can't accept your hair exactly the way it is, to me that's a form of self-hate.

Although she agrees with Nia, Sheila's interpretation introduces the idea that there are cases in which altering the self is okay, though never in the case of hair. Whereas she can see how crooked teeth may effect one's day-to-day existence, such an exception is not extended to hair. Yet if, in fact, hair alteration fosters an insidious self-hatred, then, by definition, black women who alter their hair are acting in the belief that on some level their daily lives could be affected in negative ways unless they straighten their hair. The comments by Nia and Shelia illustrate that black women still have to deal with the mental chains of slavery and Jim Crow that are exacerbated by mainstream standards of beauty that black women, in general, cannot meet. Considering the comments in chapter 1 about media and mainstream representations of beauty in U.S. society, these women explained the logical outcome of hair alteration. That is, black women are no longer held in submission by chains, nor by segregation, yet images of beauty in U.S. society are stacked against them. And they get the message loud and clear, even if they can't hear it.

Agreeing with Nia and Sheila, Elantra discussed self-hatred as existing on the subconscious level. She also introduced personality and assimilation as an influence on hair alteration, and debunked the idea that straight hair is quick, simple, and easy.

ELANTRA: I agree, but I think it's very, very subconscious. And I think it also has to do with a personality difference. Like if you want to fit in or if you just don't care what people think at all. I think it takes a lot of time to straighten hair, a lot of energy to keep it up and everything. I think that if you go through that much, then you're definitely trying to do something. It has to relate to society because it doesn't relate to you and what's most convenient for yourself. So I think it is an expression of how you relate to society and where you stand as far as trying to fit in or not liking [natural hair].

Unlike other women who perceive straight hair as easier to manage,[3] Elantra argues that hair alteration is related to fitting in, and that going natural will not gain one entrance into many circles. She also points out that if black women invest so much time and energy in their hair, then their actions can be related to their desire to fit in. Her point also begs the question that if some black women invest a lot of time and energy in their hair, particularly with regard to straightening it, does it automatically mean they are engaging in self-hating behavior? Or are there moments when hair alteration may actually be empowering for black women?

Like Elantra, Andaiye addressed how images relate to self-hatred but used a personal account to discuss her position. Like Nia and Sheila, she also provides a picture of the insidious nature and socialization process that inform how black women interpret their hair vis-à-vis white women's.

ANDAIYE: I think it can be a manifestation of [self-hatred]. I wanted the whole, you know, the long hair, the get in the water and bring your hair up and it's slicked back. But of all those things I was mimicking, they weren't of any sistas, you know what I'm saying. They were white women. So when I look at it like that, I guess it was self-esteem problems, a certain level of self-hatred. Because maybe if I had saw a sista with an Afro on that commercial and all the water sucked up in the hair, I'd have been wantin' that.

Andaiye is willing to consider that maybe self-hatred played a hand in her perception of whom she emulated when she was younger. The visibility of white women vis-à-vis black women in media images indicates the extent to which low self-esteem simmers in the conscious and subconscious psyche of many blacks. The idea that images of those who are considered beautiful and worthy of praise affect how people view themselves is not new. But without those images, individuals often weigh their worth in relationship to *some* type of other. Individuals and groups often gauge their identity in relationship to those who are not like them, which can provide insight and understanding of who they are and how they fit into society. Although Andaiye was mimicking white women in those moments of "performance," she was learning a lesson about herself and about the countless black women who know they don't have the same hair texture as white women. Andaiye's comments show that the internalization of messages in a society in which the privilege of whiteness is insidious can shape not only black people's perceptions, but whites' as well. Images of beauty in U.S. society are stacked in favor of whites; and they, too, get the message loud and clear, even if they can't hear it.

Mixed Opinions on the Self-Hatred Theory

Some of the women had mixed opinions on hair alteration as self-hatred. They argued that a more contextual approach should be used to explore the subject. The following themes, which demonstrate the diversity of thought among the women, emerged: manageability and images, choice, tradition, construction of straight as convenient or better, style, attracting mates, and alteration as a means to look one's best. Even within the individual themes, differences surfaced among the responses. For example, Kaliph based her comments on a general notion of intent.

KALIPH: I would say to the question of self-hate, I think that depends on intent. So, I relax my hair because "what?" Because I know plenty of people who relax their hair not so much because they say they hate their hair, but because it's more manageable, it's easier to comb, they like the texture of it better. By the same token, yeah, there are people who I think self-hate is an issue. "I don't like my hair because it's just too nappy, it's too kinky." I think it all boils down to intent with the self-hate question. Why you're doing what you're doing and I think there are unconscious as well as conscious acts that we do that govern our decision. An unconscious example [would be], not to undermine the women who say, "I get a relaxer because my hair is more manageable," because I believe them on their words. But then I question, how much did growing up and [ideas about] length effect the decision of what is attractive? Because it's all based on what is attractive, what looks good, these standards of beauty.

Kaliph's discussion of intent begs the question of her final comments about unconscious acts. If hair alteration for some black women is an act of unconscious self-hate, then how does intent figure in this analysis? Intent implies that the individual has an understanding of some type of means to an end. Intent also implies that one is making a *conscious* decision or is participating in a well-designed and thought-out conscious act because one is aware and desires the consequences that will follow. But like conscious acts, subconscious acts are intentional and they motivate behavior as well. In an attempt to distinguish between conscious and subconscious intent, Kaliph misses how both of these forms of intent yield the same results: an understanding and acting out of what is considered beautiful.

In addition, if Kaliph can understand how socialization fosters self-hatred when black women feel that their hair is too "kinky" or "nappy," why is her position different in those cases in which black women explain that they relax their hair for purposes of manageability? Kaliph understands the "significance" and "validity" of hair straightening in cases of manageability, but she does not address how manageability is constructed and how black women are socialized to understand that relaxed hair is manageable and natural hair is not. Though combing kinky or nappy hair can be a real issue, when the *idea* or the construction of manageability enters the social realm, it takes on a meaning and understanding that goes beyond the mere act of combing—manageability is the larger concern. By questioning the validity of the self-hatred theory through a discussion of intent, Kaliph attempts to dismiss the theory in some cases. Still, she reinforces the self-hatred theory by relating it to intent.

Ronnie also addressed the issue of intent when she decided to relax her hair.

RONNIE: It could be true in some cases but I know it's not true in all cases. As I mentioned earlier, those women who hate themselves or hate their hair and get the perms to look different or so that their hair will look different, that's definitely the case for them. For myself, I know one time I got a perm and that was for a couple of reasons. One was to prove to my mom that I was grown and I could do what I wanted. And another reason was just for experimentation, just to see what it was like.

Ronnie's reasons for relaxing her hair are grounded in ideas about rebellion and experimentation. Her intent in straightening her hair was to exhibit resistance to her mother's authority, as well as trying out relaxed hair for purposes of adornment. Ronnie's intent not only challenges the self-hatred theory, but demonstrates how broader issues influence hairstyling practices among black women. In this case, Ronnie used her hair as a way to assert her independence, which is not unlike many black people in general, and black women in particular, during the Black Power movement. Whereas black women were rejecting dominant images of beauty that privileged straight hair and white skin, Ronnie rejected her mother's control over not just her hairstyling practices, but her life in general.

Andrea presses her hair and provided a point of view that questions the very validity of self-hatred interpretations of hair alteration among black women.

ANDREA: Well, first of all, I think that a lot of those methods of altering your hair makes it easier to manage for some women. And then also I've heard that thing about self-hatred and I don't know, because if it makes a black woman feel good about herself, then I don't know if you could call that self-hatred. And on the other hand, you could say that they're just buying into this media hype and this is how they think they're supposed to look. But I don't know. It could be a self-esteem issue [in which] they feel that's how they're supposed to look.

Although Andrea understands how self-hatred may operate, she nevertheless questioned the fact that if black women feel self-assured through hair alteration, then how can it be viewed as self-hatred? Self-hatred critiques often focus on the motivation for the act of hair alteration, but Andrea provocatively referred to the positive effect that hair alteration may have on black women—that is, black women feel good about themselves, they feel beautiful after straightening their hair. Some proponents, particularly those supporting a psychological account of the theory (Grier and Cobbs 1968), argue that black women feel as if they must alter their hair *to feel good* about themselves. Andrea's observation challenges the temporal state of self-hatred if in fact that hatred disappears once a black woman straightens her hair. Andrea's idea is powerful if in fact hair alteration is really a means to an end, as an empowering moment that leads to a *greater* sense of self. Still, Andrea does say that altered hair is easier to manage, showing how altered hair is perceived in relationship to unaltered or nappy hair, and how black women perceive the material nature of hair. Semple and Isha discussed this issue as well.

Semple and Isha made very astute observations in their discussions of how relaxed or straightened hair is often associated with convenience or superiority. Although both young women touched on different ideas about the meanings of "straight" hair, the notion is still the same: straight hair is associated with positive characteristics. Semple took the issue to a different sphere, one in which the socialization of Americans often includes ingrained ideas about expedience, and how socialization shapes meanings of hair among black women in particular.

SEMPLE: I think that there are people who fall under that category definitely. I've run across women who do not fall under that category. I think the one thing that we forget when we're having this discussion about hair is that as Africans in America, we're very American, and there are certain things that are just American that we want to do. And one of those is having things the way we want to have them. And that means having things easier at times. And so along with the certain mind colonization, if you will call it that, there's this need to just have things quick and simple and easy. And when it comes to cosmetics, hair, for Africans in America, we think hair needs to be quick, simple, and easy. And we think quick, simple, and easy is rolling your hair up and sitting under a hair dryer and then waking up in the morning [and] then straightening it.

Like other women who shared mixed feelings about hair alteration, Semple understands how self-hatred may lead to it for some women. She sees how socialization plays a part in self-hate. But

52 instead of isolating her critique to how mainstream images of beauty shape, as she states, a "mind colonization of Africans in America," Semple also made a connection between the "easy life," which she argued is a very American ideal, and hair styling practices among black women. She grounded her argument in these practices but went beyond hair when she discussed the American desire for things that are "quick, simple, and easy." Although America was founded on the Protestant work ethic of hard work, Semple used the late twentieth century as her starting point to discuss how Americans have bought into ideas about convenience being better. For their part, black women have bought into ideas that straight hair is easier to manage, and therefore is better. Isha has challenged this perception of straightness.

ISHA: There definitely is a connection [with] how we feel about ourselves and putting perms in our hair and thinking that to have it straighter is to have it better. To have it straighter is to have it straighter. That's it, you know what I'm saying, like nothing more, nothing less. But like to have it straighter is to have it better is not [true].

Isha understands the foundation on which much of self-hatred theory stands: the idea that straight hair is better. Not just better in and of itself, but better in relationship to natural, tightly coiled black hair. In challenging Andrea's statement that altered hair is easier to manage, Isha not only challenged the material superiority of straightened hair, but her critique is also waged against mainstream notions of beauty and the belief that white ideas of beauty are indeed the standard. Similar as well as different ideas about whiteness in relationship to hair alteration also surfaced in the comments below.

Women with mixed feelings discussed emulating the white standard and explained the influence of choice and tradition. They also considered historical shifts in the beauty culture of black women. For example, Debra views hair alteration as a choice, but she also illustrates how self-hatred can be a factor.

DEBRA: To a certain degree, I think there is this interesting emulation of straight hair. Now, do I think it's overt self-hatred?

No, I don't think so. I think it's a choice that you're making, and it may be because I relax my hair I have a bias, but I don't think I'm [acting out self-hatred] because it's easier to do my hair this way. So a part of it is I want to look good and in it's natural state, it would take me twice as long to do my hair. So I choose this. That could be like a cop-out or something, but I [also] think there is some underlying tone in it because there is the issue of [wanting hair] bone straight. It's just how I've always grown up. I had my hair pressed, and then I had it re-laxed. I don't think it's overt to the point that it's psychologi-cally damaging. Maybe back when Madame C. J. Walker was coming' up with the pressing comb, she had some issues going' on there, so she might have started this whole thing about emulating and we pick it up and we just go on with it. You never know if it's the cause, or just "that works for me, and I'm going to keep on doing it." Yeah, we're chemically al-tering our hair but it's the same thing as getting plastic sur-gery. I think that the literature or general belief is that when you do alter something [from] its natural state, [it] points to some type of issues with your identity. So to some degree it may, but I don't think I feel that way personally.

Debra is the only woman with relaxed hair who said she might be biased in rejecting the self-hatred theory because her hair is al-tered. If in fact black women are acting out self-hatred when they alter their hair, she does not see it as being on a conscious level. By bringing in the issue of plastic surgery, she makes an extreme comparison. Debra also argues that maybe during the earlier part of the twentieth century when Madame C. J. Walker introduced the pressing comb to black women, then self-hatred may have been an issue. But now she feels, similar to Cheryl below, that hair straightening is part of the knowledge base that frames what black women know about hairstyling practices.

CHERYL: I don't think you can go as far to say you're acting out self-hatred. I mean, maybe way back when those things were first starting with black women, maybe then you could say that because those women were trying to change the way their hair had been for generations and hundreds of years.

Maybe the first women who did this might have hated the way they looked and wanted to change and look more like white people. But now I feel like it's just like tradition. Now it's like part of our culture and we've kind of adopted it. It may have had a negative history, but I think now it's just kind of part of us and an option.

Both Cheryl and Debra see tradition as a big factor in the straightening of hair by black women. Though black women who did not have a history of straightening their hair before the early twentieth century may have viewed their tightly coiled or nappy hair as undesirable, contemporary black women may not feel the same. However, tradition relates to the transmission of knowledge, opinions, customs, or practices from generation to generation. Therefore, if women in earlier generations were in fact acting out a form of self-hatred, then the idea is not far-fetched that, while transmitting the practice of hair straightening to their daughters, women also transmitted the belief that nappy hair is not attractive.

Nevertheless, Debra and Cheryl make a highly provocative observation by discussing how ideas and practices change over time. The shifts that occur within cultural practices support how meanings of hairstyling practices among black women may mean one thing at one point in time and something else later. Even within traditions, ideas and practices change to accommodate and usher in new generations that put their own spin on customs. But what about origins, which are associated with notions of authenticity and truth? Is the notion that Debra and Cheryl point to—that hair alteration is perceived differently among contemporary black women—valid? Do these practices ultimately reinforce the ideas, whether subtly or overtly, of hair alteration as a form of self-hatred during Madame C. J. Walker's time, but not in the late twentieth century? This is an important question because on one level, Debra's and Cheryl's critiques easily dismiss the self-hatred notion by separating the practice of straightening from what they see as its initial connection with black women's self-hatred and their emulation of whiteness. But on another level, it demonstrates how some black women with altered hair may rationalize their attempt not only to reject the self-hatred theory in general, but they may also rationalize their motives for altering their own hair. Though Debra says that she may be biased in her rejection of the self-hatred theory, she does not believe it applies to women of her generation, or to her personally. Both Debra and Cheryl also see hair alteration as a choice for black women.

Although other women discussed choice as well, Indigo approached it in a different way. She has mixed feelings on the subject of hair alteration as a form of self-hatred.

INDIGO: I'm mixed on it. I think that it could be internalized oppression in one sense because somehow we don't feel like we have an option of having it natural. It would be one thing if there was a choice, but I think most of us believe in order for us to succeed and to have men be attracted to us, etc., that we need to do something to our hair. And for thirteen years of my life I did that with my hair. And I think at the same level that we come from a culture, a history, an African tradition where we're able to do a lot of different things to our hair, and this is part of who we are. But I think when women decide to perm their hair it's not because they have options but because they feel like this is the only way to fit in and to feel beautiful.

Though Indigo has mixed feelings on the subject of hair alteration as self-hatred, she tends to see the issue as one of a lack of choices among black women regarding hair grooming. She understands that adorning one's hair has roots in African tradition, but she does not deny how psychology can shape black women's hairstyling practices. On the contrary, she suggests that something else is going on, too; that is, women feel they have no choice due to messages about how they should look to fit in or be beautiful.

Lee, who wears her hair in an Afro, discusses issues of style as being a possible motivation for hairstyling practices in general and straightening hair in particular, but she explained how self-hatred may be a factor for some women.

LEE: That's hard to say because it depends on what type of styles you want. Somebody might like natural styles so they keep their hair natural. Somebody might like a style that calls for straightened hair, so they get their hair straightened. It has nothing do with "oh, I hate myself and my black hair." I think the issues can be deep, but sometimes people put too much on things, rather than it might just be a face-value thing. But I guess it can get to some things where some people do not like their hair and want it to be like white people, Latino people, whatever, with straight hair. Some people have gone through struggles and things and prejudices and racism in their life, and they want to have nothing to do with black people. And this is one way [they] know [they] can control [how they] don't have to look like people like [themselves] with Afros, natural hair.

Lee is clearly critical of such analyses of self-hatred because hair-styling practices often involve adornment, period. Still, she devotes most of her discussion to explaining how hair alteration "can be that deep," meaning that it may be associated with self-hatred and not that adornment and esthetics may often influence how black women style their hair. She discusses racism and how black people internalize negative ideas and images about themselves in a society that privileges whiteness. As a result, some black people's internalization is so great that they detach themselves from anything relating to blackness, including hairstyles like the Afro that are read as "black."

Esthetics and adornment surface in Ebony's response as well. She has a texturizer and wears her hair straight. To her, hair alteration means looking one's best.

EBONY: I used to, especially this summer. I struggled a lot with that theory because up until this summer it had been like maybe nine years [since] I'd had a perm and my hair was just natural. And so I'm like I don't want to do anything with my hair. I don't want to give in to the man, I don't [want to] give in to the system. I can be natural. But then I'm like, but I only know how to care for my hair and look my best when I have some kind of chemical on it. And I want to put my best foot forward and so it's not about who dictates what I can and can't do with my hair, but it's about putting my best foot forward and looking my best, which makes me happy. So I've decided that since this is my hair and I can do whatever I want with it, that I was going to put a chemical in it because then I could look my best. So I don't think that it really has anything to do with self-hatred unless you take it to the extreme. If it's just a means to achieve a nice look, then I don't find anything wrong with it.

Ebony not only personalizes her response, but also addresses the political meanings of hair as well as ownership and property. Her comments show that personal and political ideas about the meaning of hairstyling practices among black women are often in conflict. For example, Ebony discusses how she didn't want to "give in to the man, give in to the system" by chemically altering her hair. This is important because it demonstrates how ideas about hair alteration are often translated into beliefs about cultural identity and, in this instance, selling out. She does not want to give in to the kinds of mainstream social pressures that often deny her perception that natural hair is a form of black cultural and political expression. She decided that what is often perceived in political terms is an individual issue. Therefore, like blacks in the early part of the twentieth century (Tyler 1990), she has redefined the meaning of hair alteration as a way to look her best. Still, her comments are riddled with contradiction.

Ebony's first comment is that it has been nine years since she had put chemicals in her hair; yet she can do her hair, and by extension look her best, only when she uses chemicals. Does this mean that she didn't feel she was "putting her best foot forward" during those nine years? Because looking one's "best" means having straight hair, would Ebony and others who share her position feel good about their hair, and therefore themselves, in a world without a pressing comb and relaxers? Though Ebony may know that when she straightens her hair it may be perceived as selling out, she does not see that her perception of what she feels is looking her best is related to cultural and social forces.

Despite the contradictions of Ebony's comments, the fact that she attempts to depoliticize black hairstyling practices and take ownership of what is her property speaks to empowerment. Even in the face of mainstream notions of beauty and intraracial notions of the relationship between natural hair and embracing a positive black identity, Ebony goes against the grain of nationalist and psychological readings of hair alteration. This point was also apparent in Isha's comments below.

Although Isha addressed issues that already surfaced in the earlier comments by other women, she made some interesting statements about hair and its relationship to identity. To illustrate her point, she used (dread) locking as an example.

ISHA: I think that there are definitely some black women that are like that. I don't think that you can define someone by what's on their head if they're not connected to it, number one. So it's really hard because there are sisters with locks that didn't lock their hair for the correct reasons, you know what I'm saying. So they still have issues that they're dealing with, low self-esteem or whatever and it's reflected in their hair. Some sisters that are light-skinned that lock their hair because they want to seem more black, you know what I'm saying. And that's not correct. That's not why you lock your hair. But I think it's true, that some sisters are affected by like what society says that's beautiful and therefore they would never even think of wearing their hair natural because they think that it's ugly. But there are other sisters that aren't connected to that; that think their hair is beautiful and just like their hair permed, and that's what they gon' do.

In her discussion of the "correct" reasons to lock hair, Isha demonstrates how black hair and hairstyles are policed. This is a political "correctness" that is often espoused by nationalists, leading Ebony, for example, to struggle with the decision to straighten her hair. This tension relates to ideas that advocate "correctness" because of a certain definition of authentic blackness. While this is an important point in demonstrating how hair is associated with identity, Isha has also made a more nuanced observation. She argued that if in fact black women are not connected to their hair within some cultural, political, or spiritual context,[4] then they cannot claim or accept an identity that supports accounts of self-hatred associated with hair alteration. Although Isha believes that for some women self-hatred is an issue, she questions the self-hatred claim in a distinct way. If a black

woman does not have a positive perception of her hair, whether 59
her hair is altered or natural, it is not valid to say she suffers from
self-hatred or any other identity problem. In other words, if a
black woman isn't connected to her hair in a positive way, then
she can't be accused of internalizing mainstream images of beauty.
Isha does not completely reject the self-hatred theory because she
maintains that some black women act out self-hatred when they
alter their hair.

Jean also discussed the tensions that arise among blacks when
they relate hair alteration to rejecting blackness. She also talked
about how choosing a mate can shape a black woman's decision to
alter her hair. Although most people believe that women groom
themselves to be attractive to men, few of the interviewees discussed this issue, though Jean did.

JEAN: I think it's true on a certain level. And I've asked women
about that who want to make their hair bone straight. They
claim they're not trying to not be black. But part of it I think
is pressure from the whole male-female thing. If you look at
who men are choosing, it seems as if they're choosing women
who have the long hair. And so it's not so much always self-
hatred as what is attractive to get the opposite sex. Although I
think some are self-hatred, I don't think of it as self-hatred as
much as I think of it as confusion.

Although she thinks that the self-hatred theory has credibility on
some level, Jean sees the issue as being related more to women's
"confusion" because of their desire to win the favors of men. She
feels that men are choosing women with longer, straighter hair.
Therefore, women succumb to this perceived pressure, which
often stems from "confusion," not self-hatred. Many women who
have mixed feelings about relating hair alteration to self-hatred
may feel that there is something to hair alteration that goes beyond style and is not self-hatred. Thus, why do terms like "confusion," "lack of self-acceptance," and "lack of self-love" replace
the term "self-hatred"? Perhaps it is because "hatred" is such an
extreme word. Yet, on another level, these terms may merely be re-
statements of the word "self-hatred." The idea may be couched in
different ways, but it does not change what "self-hatred" means.

The women who disagreed with the self-hatred theory based their opinion on the following points: personal satisfaction, preference, personal choice, improving the self/self-love, tradition, manageability, conformity, the oversimplification of the self-hatred theory, emulation of whiteness,[5] and a lack of self-acceptance. Most of the responses focused on manageability, emulation of whiteness, conformity, and improving the self. Women with mixed opinions made the same points on the issue as those who completely disagreed with the self-hatred argument.

Most of the women who disagreed with the self-hatred theory argued that to them the issue was manageability. Charlene discussed the related issue of versatility.

CHARLENE: Once you straighten it, you can do more things with it, different styles. You have a wider range of ways to wear it. I don't think it's not wanting to be black at all, especially certainly not in my case.

Charlene's comments and others who responded in a similar fashion explicitly define relaxed hair as versatile, with the unruliness of kinky or nappy hair always being implicit. Relaxed or straightened hair is seen as manageable and versatile in comparison to nappy hair. This was a point underscored by Stephanie.

STEPHANIE: [Black women] shouldn't hate themselves if they have nappy hair or curly hair or whatever. 'Cause I know I don't. I just put a relaxer on my hair because by it being nappy, [I] couldn't do nothin' with it.

Like Stephanie and Cheryl, all of the women who rejected the self-hatred account of hair alteration personalized their response by stating that although they wear their hair relaxed, it is not due to any self-hatred.

Women who discussed the relationship between emulating whiteness and hair alteration also gave personalized accounts. Three of the four women who addressed emulating whiteness also relax their hair, as, for example, Keisha.

KEISHA: Well I don't think I hate myself because I relax my hair. To me, I just do it because, well, I like it straighter. That's all, really. I think it's easier to manage for me right now being straight and shorter. Eventually I want to move to where it's even shorter than it is just for, you know, maintenance purposes. But in no way for me is it a self-hatred kind of deal where I'm just like, "oh I gotta be the white girl or I gotta have this bone-straight hairdo to fit in" or anything like that.

Keisha and some of the other women translate self-hatred into meaning an attempt to look white, and they reject such an argument. DuCille (1996) rejects the "desire to be white" argument as well, but she provides a more insidious reading of what black girls and women feel denotes privilege:

> Image experts such as the authors of *The Color Complex: The Politics of Skin Color among African Americans* maintain that "countless Black girls in the United States share the fantasy of becoming White." "How could it be otherwise," they ask, "in a society whose ideal beauty—blonde, pale skinned, with blue eyes—embodies everything the average Black female lacks?"
>
> Despite the hue of my own girlhood fantasies, I would argue the subtle but essential point that there may be much more to a black girl's dreaming white than the desire to be white and the self-hatred such dreams are assumed to imply. For a child—particularly a black child growing up in the absence of colored images—dreaming white is the natural response to what the child sees and does not see in society's looking glass. The absence of black images in the "social mirror" leaves the black child with little other than white subjects for self-reflection and self-projection. But a child's dreaming in the color scheme privileged by the world around her is not necessarily the same as wanting *to be* that color.
>
> However large he may have loomed in my daydreams, Glen Evans was never a way for me to imagine *myself* white. Nor was his presence in my fantasy life a sign that my child's

62 mind had bought the postwar myth of a raceless, great society where white men reigned beneficent under the doctrines of a colorblind Constitution. I knew I was black and female, and I was too much my mother's daughter not to be in some way fiercely proud of that fact. But I also sensed at an early age the consequences of my color and my gender. What guided my fantasy life, I believe, was less a wish to flee my own black flesh than a desire to escape the limitations that went with such bodies. (pp. 12–13)

Like duCille's association of privilege with white skin, the women who focused on the "emulation of whiteness" point related it to manageability and to the perceived hairstyling practices of white women, not necessarily to their desire to be white. Because Keisha and other women chose to discuss hair alteration within the context of manageability and whiteness, we can assume that to many black women straight hair is perceived as manageable and is often associated with white women. Keisha stated matter-of-factly that she prefers her hair straight, but we must remember that individual preference is often shaped by broader social and cultural forces. Though actual self-hatred may be far-fetched, these women's ideas do not spring from a vacuum.

Other women focused on still broader forces that can influence black women's decisions to straighten their hair. Raine discussed social and economic pressures faced by black women, and Taylor added that hairstyling practices are often guided by economic necessity.

RAINE: I don't think its self-hatred. I think it's being able to fit in easily. If you leave you hair [natural] for instance, men will tell me that [they] like a woman that is natural. Natural hair, natural nails, natural everything. And I say, "what do you think about Whoopi Goldberg?" "Uhh, God, her hair!" That's natural. But they look down on it, they frown upon it, they cannot stand it. They want that white-girl straight look. The jobs want the white-girl straight look.
TAYLOR: I wouldn't think of it in terms of self-hatred. I would think of it in terms of you have to do what you have to do to get over and the white man does what he has to do to get

over, and why should we not do the same thing? We're all out
there economically trying to compete for the dollars, so by
whatever means necessary that's what it's all about. So you
have to go with the flow. . . . There's so many things that they
nit-pick at black women or men until [you take the position]:
"Look, clone yourself like them. Go in there, come home [and]
do whatever you have to do to enjoy yourself at home." That's
what you have to do but you still have to earn a living.

These comments reveal that black women receive messages that
guide an understanding that straight hair is privileged in the social as well as occupational arena. Raine and Taylor believe that a
"white look" fosters not self-hatred, but shows the lengths that
black people in general, and black women in particular, have to
go to in order to succeed. This feeling was very prominent during
the early part of the twentieth century when many African Americans associated acceptable or appropriate grooming practices
with succeeding in life (Tyler 1990). Moreover, the way in which
"white" is associated with success demonstrates how ideas about
hair are linked to ideas that intersect with race, and with economic and romantic success. In turn, these ideas shape black
women's understanding about how they must negotiate their marginal position in a racist and sexist society.

Still, Raine's and Taylor's statements relay a sense of empowerment. Taylor used the words of Malcolm X when she stated that
black women must succeed "by any means necessary," which in
this case means "getting over," because that's what white people
do. Therefore, proponents of the self-hatred theory argue against
hair alteration. Black women, and black people in general, understand that knowledge of how "to get over" will lead to occupational and economic success. What could be more empowering?

Some of the women I interviewed actually defined hair alteration as an empowering act, though their comments are not without contradiction. For example, Mrs. Franklin discussed improving her looks and dressing well, but insisted she was not trying
to emulate whiteness when altering her hair.

MRS. FRANKLIN: I would say to them, I'm not trying to do
anything to look like a white person. I'm trying to improve

my looks, not taking after a white person or trying to be like a white person. I think if your hair is not in order then you not well dressed. Your hair has to be in order to be well dressed.

Though Mrs. Franklin may be trying to improve her looks, her statement presumes that there was something wrong with her looks before she straightened her hair. Grooming one's hair seems to be central to bringing some type of order or discipline to the body. Although Mrs. Franklin adamantly challenges the self-hatred theory, her comment about "improving" herself, even if it is self-empowering, still shows that she understands the relationship between improving oneself and getting rid of kinky or nappy hair.

Kim, who wears her hair relaxed, and Laurie, who wears a short natural style, went beyond Mrs. Franklin's challenge to the self-hatred theory by discussing self-love. But Kim's statement echoed Mrs. Franklin's to some extent:

KIM: Self-hatred, I wouldn't say that. I think for me it's the love of myself. I want to better myself. I want to maximize my appearance as best that I can and work with what I have. So for me, it's not a hatred towards myself. It's more I love myself [and] I want to use what I have to project that and work on that.

Kim's goal to "maximize her appearance" exists on a continuum with Mrs. Franklin's ideas about "improving her looks." Because Kim gives more voice to loving herself and even employs the term "self-love," she challenges the self-hatred account. Laurie's words take the rejection further.

LAURIE: I think that it does foster insecurity to a certain extent. I went to this shop and I was like, "cut it off." And when I looked in the mirror and it was like, wow. But even when I cut it, I wasn't totally satisfied. It was like, there's something missing. Three days later I was like, "I'm gonna dye my hair." But who actually can determine if that's self-hatred? Maybe God gave us this hair for us to create with and feel with and lend emotion to and be mad when it doesn't look like you

want it to. And maybe it's a lesson in all of that. So I can't really say if it fosters self-hatred, that's so severe. If anything,
I've learned to love myself more over the years with my hair
being shorter even though I've gone through the drama of
perming and all kinds of [things]. I would say insecurity for
some, but maybe not hatred.

Laurie restates the issue as having to do with insecurity. She
feels the self-hatred theory is severe because there are some issues that involve the self, but there is still a distinction between
hatred and insecurity. This is yet another example of how several of the women try to challenge the self-hatred argument by
using terms that appear to be less harsh or judgmental than
"self-hatred." They challenge the *terminology* of "self-hatred,"
but "insecurity" does not completely challenge the *idea* of self-
hatred. However, Laurie does challenge the self-hatred theory
when she speculates about the utility of hair. This statement is
a direct challenge and deconstruction of the self-hatred theory.
Laurie suggests that it may have been God's will and desire to
have humans adorn their hair, play with it, be emotional about
it. She supports the adornment argument and its connection to
African cultural practices (Sagay 1983). She provided room for a
reading of hair alteration as being connected to disliking the
self, but ultimately she sees it as a loving of the self. By using
herself as an example, Laurie describes how she has come to
love herself to an even greater extent by doing her hair in several ways, including straightening it.

Mariya also used different terminology in her discussion. She
replaced self-hatred with a lack of self-acceptance.

MARIYA: I wouldn't necessarily call it self-hatred but I think
that when [a] wom[a]n gets to a point where you're burning
yourself and getting other injuries, it's a lack of self-acceptance. Because I think there's a lot of women who have no idea
of what their hair would look like naturally; who haven't had
a perm in their hair since they were kids and just can't stand
the way that their natural hair really looks. I wouldn't go so
far as to say self-hatred because I think there are other things
that women might hate about themselves more. I think that

66   maybe body type or for some black women maybe our skin tone.

By explaining how body type and skin color may be considered as fostering *more* self-hate among black women, Mariya likewise gives credence to (self) hate. A lack of self-acceptance presumes a rejection of the self in some fashion, which can be related to some form of hate. Although she tries to reject self-hatred in connection with hair alteration, Mariya's statement still supports it when she explains that some women despise their hair in its natural state. Laurie discusses adornment and creativity as motivations for hair alteration, thereby leaving room for empowerment.

Like Laurie and Mariya, Charlene also does not see hair alteration among black women as a sign of self-hatred. However, unlike the other women, she discussed hair straightening among black women as something habitual and justified her practice of straightening her hair.

CHARLENE: I strongly disagree with that point of view. I'm very happy with myself. I love myself. Like I said, sometimes I do wear my hair natural, but I think that's just being brought up in America. It's very hard to change after thirty years and go, "okay, I'm not going to straighten my hair anymore" when [that's] all you've known. It's more like habit and what you've been taught to do. I don't think it's any form of self-hatred.

Charlene explained how growing up in American society shapes black women's actions on a daily basis. Yet she does not question how habits are learned through socialization. What she described as a habit derived from being brought up in America may be more telling than she realizes: growing up in America may indeed shape black women's habits given the images of beauty they see in the media.

Dianne, who wears her hair relaxed, strongly felt that hair alteration did not mean self-hatred. Like Mrs. Franklin, she addressed the emulation of whiteness argument, saying it is often attached to self-hatred. By personalizing her position, she argued that hair alteration is linked to her desire to look nice.

DIANNE: Well, I think it's awful [to think that if black women
straighten their hair then they hate themselves or they are
trying to look white]. I think you can do anything within
your capability, financially or whatever, to improve the way
you look. I don't see anything wrong with it. I don't think
when I straighten my hair or perm my hair I'm trying to be
white. I'm just trying to look better for me, and not for my
husband, my friend, or nobody else. For *me.*

Although Dianne may groom her hair only to please herself, there
is still an understanding that straight hair looks *better,* and "better" is used in comparison to kinky or nappy hair. In other words,
straight hair is always "better" than tightly coiled black hair. Dianne does not take into account that if something is "better," it is
better than *something else,* in this case tightly coiled hair.

Barbara, who wears her hair relaxed, discussed hair alteration
as a personal preference that involves style.

BARBARA: Definitely no self-hatred, by no means. It's a preference. What you want as a woman, what you want personally.
Whether you want the braids, the straight, back into a natural, whatever. That's a preference.

Barbara describes different types of hairstyles but, unlike those
who alter their hair because of manageability or because they just
like it a certain way, Barbara expresses preference in ways that
emphasize choice and she hints at adornment practices. As a result, her rejection of the self-hatred theory relates to ideas about
the self as a determined agent in control of her thoughts and
actions.

Stacy felt that the self-hatred account of hair alteration is sim-
plistic, and her comments place her among those who reject the
self-hatred theory. She also placed the discussion within broader
ideas about womanhood, that the message to all women is that
they are deficient in some way and need to change something
about themselves. The issue of women altering their bodies is important for understanding how all women are influenced by societal messages, and how cross-cultural analyses of womanhood are
often valid. However, Stacy challenged the inherent problems

that arise when *intracultural* constructions of identity fail to capture the complexity of individuals.

STACY: My first response would be, that's totally overly simplified because human beings are more complex than that. So, it's a range of factors influencing what people do on a day-to-day basis. I've known women who have permed hair who I think are more like at peace with themselves and grounded in their history and black people. And then there are people with locks who treat you worse than white people would treat you. I think we're dealing with a lot of cognitive distortion and dissonance that is endemic to the larger society 'cause all the messages [relay that] whether you are like Christie Brinkley or one of us, there's something wrong with you and you need to fix yourself on a daily basis. And even if you are skinny and blonde, you still walk around with that feeling of lack. So I think if anything it's more of a systemic issue than individual black women hating themselves and getting perms.

Stacy's cross-cultural analysis is more detailed than Habiba's (chapter 1). Habiba confined her comments to hair specifically, but Stacy uses hair as a basis for discussing how women feel about themselves in relation to media images. Instead of stating that white women also have problems with their hair, as Habiba had done, Stacy fleshed out the issue and makes the observation that women are socialized to feel they need to make themselves over. Confining the self-hatred critique to black women fails to consider the fact that all women alter their body in some way and that these acts say more about the kind of society we live in than about individual acts of perceived self-hatred among black women. What does all this mean for black women's understanding about choice, power, and femininity in relationship to hair? Chapter 3 examines these issues and related ones.

Splitting Hairs

Power, Choice, and Femininity

An important critique of the self-hatred account of hair alteration is that it does not take into consideration hairstyling practices that reflect how black women exercise power and choice, as some women noted in chapter 2. The possibility that hairstyling practices, in whatever form, serve as a challenge to mainstream notions of beauty or that they allow black women to embrace a positive identity is important for two reasons: voice and empowerment. Voice is important for marginalized groups in U.S. society, and it is through voice that black women are not merely victims of oppression. Instead, black women are agents or thinking and acting beings who understand the forces that shape their lives. This chapter continues to engage several issues that emerged in previous chapters, and introduces other issues as well.

Hair and Power

Is hair associated with power in any way? After posing this question to my interviewees, I explained power could be viewed from the girls' and women's own perspective. As a result, the responses were more insightful than if I had given them only one definition of power, or only one way of approaching the question. They were thus able to address the question on their own terms. For example, they addressed topics ranging from hair and power, hair as empowerment, natural hair as empowerment, hair as disempowerment, hair as economic power, hair texture as power, hair as power to attract mates, and hair as power to support perceptions and stereotypes.

The women who discussed the relationship between hair and power did so in a variety of ways. Ronnie provided a very concise explanation by addressing the issue within a general framework of loving the self and power.

RONNIE: I think that anyone who loves their self for who they are and doesn't really care what anyone thinks is powerful. Now, if that's wearing a perm, wearing locks, wearing braids, whatever it is. As long as you're happy within yourself and you can say I'm truly happy, then that's powerful.

Ronnie's point relates to being true to one's self and how such truth transforms into happiness. The very act of self-definition renders power. This is a very important point in relationship to black women and their ability to define their own realities, and it relates to power. Furthermore, Ronnie challenged meanings of hairstyling practices: instead of perceiving some hairstyles as representing power (e.g., the Afro) and others as disempowerment (e.g., straightened hair), to her the ability to make decisions in the face of rejection is powerful. In other words, instead of hairstyling practices as the site of tension, Ronnie shifted the discussion to an explanation about the relationship between power and self-definition.

Lisa's point was similar to Ronnie's in the sense that she discussed the power of going against the grain. Yet Lisa also explained how hair and hairstyles have the ability to make personal statements that can be translated into power.

LISA: I think that it can be. I just think that a woman is a powerful being, and if she can like use her hair as a means, as a tool to have power. Like if it goes with her business suit or whatever, she may want to put her hair up in a certain style. It could be like a power statement, like take me seriously or something like that. Or if you want to wear it long, or braids, or a natural, or [whatever]. It can be a personal statement and maybe it could give that individual like a sense of power, [by stating] I'm bold and confident enough that I don't have to go with the "norm" or societal way.

By discussing hair as a tool or as a way to make a statement, Lisa describes how hair has the potential to be used as a means to an end. Her comments demonstrate the potential potency of hair, particularly its ability to be used to make powerful statements. But as Lisa noted, it is what those appearances or statements mean that show the relationship between hair and power.

Isha discussed hair and power in relationship to the physical and metaphysical state of a black woman. She sees the state of one's hair as a narrative that says something about what is going on in the woman's life.

ISHA: I think it can be yes. I think for some sisters, their hair is powerful and they're powerful, so therefore everything they deal with is powerful, you know what I'm saying? I think for other [sisters], they don't have that connection with their hair because their hair is dead. . . it's not alive. Whether they've dyed it so much it's brokedown, unhealthy. Whether they're puttin' crack in their bodies and their shit ain't growin'. Whether they got 'locks but they with this man and he's beatin' on [them]. The energy that's put into it, it could be on a strictly physical level like it could just be permed, it's out of control. It could be dead because of that. But it can be permed and be very healthy and vibrant and shiny too. So I think there is power associated with it and I think when people look at like 'locks and braids, the image of that brings up for us as Africans the things associated with power, like kings and queens and beauty and grace.

Isha views hair as being potentially both powerful and disempowering. She discusses hair as "dead" not only as a result of what they do to it, but also as in terms of what they do to their bodies as a result of drug abuse, or those things that others do to their bodies through physical abuse. She also associates power with hairstyles, particularly braids and dreadlocks, and relates them to African civilization. However, Isha does not believe that these styles are the only ones that represent power because by discussing the vibrant nature of healthy, shiny permed or relaxed hair, Isha, like Lisa, provides a more inclusive reading of "alive" or powerful hair.

Several of the women specifically discussed hair in relation to empowerment, as Indigo's comment shows.

INDIGO: I think there is a certain power, for women especially. A lot of our values in terms of beauty and how we validate [who] we are, are based on hair. Whether you're white or whatever. You need to have this thick long flowing hair, that is the standard. But power, I think, for black women in choosing to have their hair natural is somewhat of a revolutionary act in a sense. It's kind of going against the grain and going against the societal standards telling you how you're supposed to look. My two sisters and my mom have perms. I have no judgment on them in terms of doing that because I had to do it for a long time, and I've reached a certain place where I choose not to do it anymore. But I feel more powerful with my hair like this and I feel more comfortable with who I am, and I think I kinda have more of a fuck-you attitude because I don't care what you feel about my hair. In fact, I'm insulted, especially when white people come up to me and say they like my hair because I've had to listen to [their] value judgments to create who I am for so long. I don't want [them] to validate or not validate me. [Their] opinion has no bearing on what I choose to do anymore.

Earlier in the interview Indigo had said that black women are taught that nappy hair is a badge of shame. But when she relates it to power, she feels that embracing tightly coiled black hair is empowering, as did Elantra in chapter 1. She does not view her hair in its natural state as disempowering, thus relating it to a broader societal *and* personal context. In agreement with Stacy's comments at the end of chapter 2, Indigo reflected on cross-cultural meanings of hair and how all women's ideas about hair help shape their overall sense of self. But she explained why these meanings, particularly in reference to natural styles are different for black women. Clearly she feels that black women who choose to wear their hair natural are participating in a revolutionary act, something that is subversive or goes against the grain of accepted ideas or practices. Furthermore, choice is important to her; it means a person has the power to make decisions. The issue of choice is important for two reasons. First, Indigo grounds her discussion of empowerment in personal experience by noting that her rejection of external validations of beauty have helped shape her hairstyling choices (practices). Her choice to reject white people's validation illustrates Indigo's firm position in refusing to accept mainstream definitions of beauty and external validations. Second, exercising choice relates to wearing one's hair natural, which in turn relates to a revolutionary practice. The importance of Indigo's use of the word "revolutionary" demonstrates hair's relationship to the broader social and political concerns of black women. Although Indigo is non-judgmental about her sister's and mother's decision to straighten their hair, she does not use the word choice. Nor does she imply a revolutionary act in relationship to straightening hair because she perceives going *against* the grain as a revolutionary act.

In a followup response to Indigo's comments, Semple also addressed empowerment. I provided Semple with some probes,[1] giving her examples of how other women addressed the question in reference to power and empowerment, and she made these comments.

SEMPLE: I think the thing that empowers one is the ability to make choices for yourself and be self-determined. So if that means that you're self-determined and you want your hair to be straight, then that can be an empowering thing for you. You can come from a whole family of people [that are] just totally against straightening your hair, processing your hair in any type of way. It can be an empowering decision to say, "You know what, I'm going to go get a perm." On the flip side, you can come from a family that says, "Process all the way." The longer the better, the straighter the better. And then it can be empowering for you to say, "Well, I'm going to wear my hair natural." So it's about the choices and your ability to make those choices that brings empowerment.

Semple extends Indigo's comments by discussing how one's ability to make choices is empowering. Semple sees the act of black women choosing to wear their hair any way they want, in the face of societal, cultural, and familial opposition, as a sign of empowerment. Unlike Indigo, for Semple the act of *choosing* is the empowering or revolutionary act. This is an important point because the idea of choice presumes some type of power that individuals can exercise. The choice to go against the grain, whatever that grain may be, is an empowering exercise in and of itself, according to Semple. She goes beyond Indigo's conception of empowerment.

Although Indigo discussed the empowerment that comes with wearing one's hair natural, her position relates to choice as well. There were other comments that related natural hair and empowerment, but they were addressed in different ways. For example, Nia commented that wearing one's hair natural is empowering.

NIA: I think it is empowering to wear natural hair, at least for me it has been, and I know it has been for other black women that I've talked with. When you finally decide to wear your hair natural there's something about the statement because really you're taking a stand and you're presenting yourself to everybody. And when you get to that point, you've already empowered yourself to make a stance.

By relating natural hair to empowerment, Nia rejects the belief that natural hair is undesirable. She also sees wearing natural hair as a statement that black women make, or one that can be read as going against the grain of mainstream images of beauty, that is, straight and straightened hair. Furthermore, Nia feels comfortable, empowered even, in personalizing her claims, an act that was riddled with ambivalence in Charlene's comments, which, although similar to Nia's, diverge once she shared her personal experience.

CHARLENE: It depends on the individual. Like if you like your hair natural and you don't wear it that way simply to fit in or something, then you feel that there is some power. Like a

woman who would wear her hair natural in the face of all this
controversy is a very strong woman, I think. But on the flip
side of that, I consider myself to be a strong woman. And I'm
definitely proud of being black, and that's why I'm just sort
of confused about why I straighten my hair, but I still do it.

Charlene's comments demonstrate how cultural ideas of what it
means to be "black" often relate to natural hair. She illustrates
how ideas about an "authentic" black identity shape the interpretation and internalization of these ideas on a personal level.
Her view of the "controversy" that surrounds natural hair is
linked to socially constructed ideas about what is beautiful and
accepted and the importance in maintaining the status quo.
Thus, "strength" in character can be measured through hair;
but tensions still exist within Charlene's understanding because, although she wears her hair straightened, she considers
herself a strong woman. She understands cultural constructions
of hair in relationship to natural hair and black pride. It is
through her own understanding in relationship to being a
strong black woman with straightened hair that provides a
clear picture of the tensions that surface in ideas about black
womanhood.

Ndeye-ante, who wears her hair in braid extensions, discussed
on a personal level how hair can be both powerful and disempowering for black women. Unlike Charlene, Ndeye-ante provided a different view of what type of hair is privileged.

NDEYE-ANTE: Yeah, I think growing up as a dark-skinned girl
with very nappy hair, my hair was never very short, but it
was never long, so it was very typical. But there was definitely power associated with the other girls, my playmates.
Even in high school and college my girlfriends and sister-
friends who had longer and straighter hair, they felt a sense of
empowerment because we adored them. We were taught too.
And not by white people directly. I mean, that was the deep
part about it. The way it works is that the white person
doesn't have to be in front of you preaching to you, "love
me better than your[self]" anymore because we teach each
other that. We get trained so well.

Ndeye-ante not only addresses how skin color and hair shape black women's sense of self, but, like Sheila and Nia in chapter 2, she explains how the process of disliking black physical features is very insidious because of mainstream images of beauty. In fact, there is a thin line that separates mainstream images of beauty and those by U.S. blacks due to "training" or internalizing oppressive ideology.[2]

She also explains how individual identity occurs in relationship to other people. Ndeye-ante came to an understanding about light skin and straight hair privilege by seeing how others treated her friends who had these characteristics. Ndeye-ante's association of the glorification of light skin and straight hair with mainstream standards of beauty illustrate how black women understand what is privileged and what is not. Indeed, slavery has ended, but the psychological scars remain, as do more subtle forms of devaluing black physical characteristics.

Laurie discussed how hair has the ability to disempower due to myths that have been perpetuated by previous generations, particularly in relationship to cutting hair.[3]

LAURIE: Yeah I do. Going back to the saying as far as your hair is your crown. And when you cut your hair, your crown is taken away. I think that many of us as black women have allowed ourselves to feed into that kind of myth and I think that the elders of our generation kind of fostered that, in a sense. And no disrespect to them.

Crown suggests a source of power, excellence, or beauty. Glory is defined as something that makes a person honored or illustrious. Glory also relates to pride, and pride to self-esteem. Pride suggests a high or inordinate opinion of one's importance as displayed through one's conduct, physical appearance, or in some other way. Therefore, a notion of power is embedded in the idea of hair as a black woman's crowning glory. Hair has the ability to become a foundation for understanding how black women view power and its relationship to self-esteem.

It is Laurie's final comment above that provides a background for understanding, at least in part, of what happened in Brooklyn at P.S. 75. When Laurie explained that older blacks have nurtured myths about hair in black communities, she illustrated through her comments that while the kids may have been excited about a book that embraced nappy hair, it was the adults who raised concerns. In the late 1960s and early 1970s, it was black youth culture that ushered in the Afro on a grand scale, much to the discomfort of many blacks from previous generations. Laurie touches on general tensions that have emerged and continue to form within black communities across the generations.

Toya discussed the relationship between hair and identity differently from Laurie. She explained that hair has an ability to "say" something about an individual, and that hairstyles are often associated with one's politics.

TOYA: I see that certain stereotypes go along with certain types of hairstyles. I notice if one has locked hair, one is assumed to be automatically a revolutionary. If one's hair is permed, one is assumed to be an accommodationist. I guess hair has power [because] it [can] cast an impression of you without saying a word. So I would say hair has power in that context.

Ideas that emerged in the 1960s about hair being a political statement still exist today in Toya's estimation. Still, she recognizes how stereotypes are only assumptions that may say absolutely nothing about one's politics. This point challenges the transference of past political definitions of hair as well as the belief that hair can be a marker of one's politics in particular and overall identity in general.

There is a statement about hair in relationship to racial identity in Toya's comments: it is not merely stereotypes that exist on one's head, whether the stereotype is couched in "revolutionary" or "accommodationist" terms, but it is what hair brings to racial stereotypes.

Hair and Choice

As some women have shown in the previous section, ideas about power relate to choice and autonomy. Therefore I asked the women to address the following question: Do black women have a choice or say in the way they wear their hair that is independent of any kind of external forces? Most of the women either agreed that black women have a choice or provided explanations that illustrate the contexts under which choice is exercised. Only a few women completely felt that black women did not have a choice or say in how they wear their hair.

The women who felt that black women have free choice discussed their position in relation to self-determination and versatility. Shannon, who wears her hair relaxed, explained how choice is independent of external forces, especially in relationship to occupation and men.

SHANNON: Yeah, we have choice how we want to wear our hair regardless of where we work or boyfriend. My boyfriend don't like the way my hair look that's his problem, not mine. Because I'm gon' wear what looks good on me, you know. I believe however you choose to wear your hair is on you [whether it's] red, black, green, cut short, long, it don't matter. I hope it's no one around here that say that their man don't want them to wear their hair some way. She needs to be schooled for real.

Shannon was adamant in her position about black women exerting autonomy with regard to hairstyling decisions. She made a feminist statement by asserting that when women make hairstyling choices, they should resist the desires of their partners. Her comment demonstrates that exercising choice is rooted within the individual.

Similarly, Barbara explained how hairstyle choice is a reflection of the person. The idea of choice remains within the individual as opposed to outside forces such as friends.

BARBARA: You have to think about yourself and what makes you happy versus what your friends [think]. Your hairstyle, whatever it is, is an expression of you as an individual.

By asserting that hairstyles are a reflection of the individual, not of one's relationship to a group, Barbara depoliticizes hair. She does not privilege "strategic essentialism" or a fixed black identity, nor does she accept stereotypes that render differences among blacks invisible. It is the individual who determines her life chances, not external forces.

But what does such a perspective mean for powerful images of black women that include Mammy, Sapphire, and Jezebel? In a society that perceives all black women as a group and not as individuals, how realistic is Barbara's position? By understanding that choice is related to power, Barbara carves out a space, if only on a personal level, where black women can exercise some choice over their lives.

Elisa, a sophomore in high school who wears her hair relaxed, extended the notion of choice but she explained her position in relationship to a choice in hairstyles.

ELISA: We have a choice about everything, including hair. You can wear your hair any way you want to wear it and you have the choice whether to relax it or wear it in braids, or put in a jheri curl. You can do anything you want to with it.

This argument relates to the versatility that many of the girls and women have already referred to. Though some view choice as it relates to power and autonomy, to others choice relates to how black women can groom their hair.

The discussions that follow address general ideas about choice. Andrea discussed the price that comes with exercising choice by providing a personal example. She related personal choice as being shaped by an understanding of the consequences that follow one's decision.

ANDREA: I think we do have a personal choice, but every choice is going to come with a price. And so it just depends on how much you're willing to say I'm going to do this and I don't care what anybody thinks. Every time I get my hair braided, I just dread going to class the next day because everybody's gonna be like, "Oh, your hair?" And you know they're wondering, "Was her hair that long or does it just look like that 'cause she braided it?" I believe that's the price, just having to explain. It's like you can do whatever

you want to your hair, but just know that somebody is
gonna make you explain. I just feel like that's a real invasion
of personal space, to have to get that deep. And then if you
don't want to explain, they think that, you know, you're trying to keep some secret from them or something. A mysterious cultural thing.

Andrea's point mirrors the concerns that many of the women and
girls expressed about the fascination of many nonblacks with
black hair and hairstyles. By mentioning the explanations that
often seem to be necessary with black hair and styles such as
braid extensions, for example, Andrea shows that there is a
"price" that black women have to pay. The "price" is an invasion
of personal space, and a reluctance to permit such an invasion is
read by nonblacks as blacks' attempt to be mysterious. Andrea's
admission that she is reluctant to explain black hairstyles to nonblacks and go to class after her hair is braided demonstrates how
black women need to negotiate the fascination of others with
black hairstyling practices. For example, after women get their
hair done, they usually look forward to the attention they will receive.[4] However, for Andrea it is different. Within intercultural
environments, the focus for many black women with braided
styles moves away from beauty and a nice hairdo: they become
representations of "mysterious" cultural practices that require
explanations.

Like Andrea, Nia discussed exercising choices and the result-
ing ramifications, but she went even further.

NIA: I absolutely believe we always have personal choice.
Whether we exercise it, we always have a say, whether we
verbalize it or not. What that means though is when you
make a personal choice you have to live with what comes
with choice. But for the most part, I think the consequences
seem more severe than they would turn out to be. I think we
can adjust to those. I think other people would adjust to
those. I think black men would adjust. I think corporate
America would adjust. If we felt strongly enough about it to
make that personal choice, which we could do, but we just
don't.

Nia sees the inability of black women to exercise choice in relationship to hairstyling practices as indicative of complacency.
Her understanding of choice is "personal," which renders the influence of broader social, cultural, and political forces invisible.
Still, she notes that external forces such as black men and corporate America have the ability to influence choice. This was clearly
the case when black women took American Airlines and Hyatt
hotels to court and defended their right to wear braids in the
workplace in the late 1980s. Nia's explanation of choice as personal therefore does not render black women powerless in shaping their lives in broader social contexts. The idea of personal
choice speaks to a type of ownership or control of one's destiny
that translates into empowerment, as the plaintiffs in the 1980s
court cases demonstrated.

Like Nia, Isha argued that black women exercise personal
choice, but she was more explicit in her discussion of how "personal" choice is influenced by external forces.

ISHA: It's like there are sisters that don't feel like they have a
personal choice and they don't exemplify that and their personal choice is completely defined by what someone else tells
them. Whether it's their mother, their lover, society, whatever.
They don't exhibit the necessary skills to have personal
choice. Everybody doesn't have that 'cause they don't see
themselves as having it. But they could, you know what I'm
saying.

Like Nia, Isha argues that black women's ability to exercise personal choices is influenced by external forces. However, they
could tap into their own abilities if they actually believed that
they *have* a choice.

Indigo agreed with Nia and Isha but she personalized her position by discussing her experiences after shaving her head.

INDIGO: I think we have a choice but I think we don't realize
we have a choice. I know when I shaved off my head and was
bald, so many black women [were] saying they wish they
could do [it] or that they felt like they didn't have the right
body size to do it. Head size, head shape, all of these different

things [are] reasons why they couldn't do it. And so I think that even though there is a choice, we don't believe there is such a choice because we are conditioned to believe that we're supposed to look a certain way.

Indigo explains how factors other than those that are external often affect the exercise of choice, particularly in relationship to women's to hairstyles that are unconventional. What does it mean when black women say, "I wish I could do that to my hair," and they use excuses that have to do with their physical appearance? Social and cultural forces that shape images of beauty overall appear to disappear, and the problem lies in another part of the body. But within these explanations, ideas about what is physically beautiful continue to be shaped by social ideas. How did the women who approached Indigo come to believe that their head is too big and that their face is not the right size to shave their head? These comments show that ideas about what is unattractive or unconventional are reinforced by excuses about one's head and face size. Such explanations of imperfections send messages of inferiority to all women. As a result, black women's ability to exercise choice becomes limited: they are conditioned or socialized to believe they must look a certain way.

Ronnie discussed socialization and how it influences black women's ability to exercise choice with regard to hairstyling practices. She also focused on choice in relationship to child-rearing practices that nurture a positive self-esteem.

RONNIE: It depends a lot on how you were brought up. Because if you were brought up to be proud of who you are and how you look, then it wouldn't matter what any outside force would have to say.

Ronnie makes two implicit assumptions here: (1) an individual's socialization occurs only among family; and (2) an individual's socialization ends once they reach adulthood. On one level, Ronnie's argument illustrates that despite societal pressure and images, black women instilled with a positive view of self can exercise choice. But by arguing that choice is dependent on how one has been raised, Ronnie denies the importance that ex-

ternal forces play on one's ability to exercise choice. Her perspective assumes that all these women can exist outside of peer
and social group networks, and be exempt from the influence of
television, movies, magazines, and other media. Although Ronnie's argument is qualitatively different from conservative readings of why black people, especially the poor, are in the state
they are in, both are linked in that they lead to a broader argument: individuals have complete control or autonomy over
their life choices. Moynihan (1965) related the problems in
black communities to the "unnatural" predominance of female-
headed households. Instead of understanding how institutions
and structures of power shape black people's lives, Moynihan
placed the blame of black failure on "dysfunctional" black behavior without even considering institutionalized racism. Ronnie made a leap that is as unsettling as Moynihan's in a broader
context of socialization and social forces.

Keisha also discussed socialization but was more specific by describing how girls are not allowed to exercise choice with regard
to hairstyling practices. She pointed out that age is important in
one's ability to exercise choice.

KEISHA: I think as you get older you might have a little bit
more choice in it, but as a child I don't think you do. Like if
it was up to me, I would have never gotten my hair pressed
as a child because it was one of the most traumatic experiences every time I would get it pressed. I was always
hunchin' up my shoulders seeing if I was gonna get burned,
you know, your mother in the back [of your neck]. [And
your mother saying], "Girl, that just the heat." [And you re-
plying], "But no, Mommy, it's on my head, you burnin' me!
That is not the heat!" So I think as a child you really don't
have any say-so in, you know, how your hair is groomed. So
as you get older, you can make more choices about how you
want to do it. But at the same time I think that certain
things do impact because I know someone who won't go to
women to get their hair done because they know what a
man likes more in a hairstyle than women. So, I think that
even when you have more control, you're still influenced by
outside factors.

Splitting Hairs

Kai, a fifteen-year-old who wears long braid extensions, explained her inability to exercise choice because her father has forbidden her to straighten her hair.

KAI: Well I think [black girls and women] should have a chance or say but [there's always something]. Like my father will not allow [me to relax my hair]. He'll get really upset [if I bring it up]. My mother said that on my sixteenth birthday if I really want too, that she'll do it anyway. I think we should have a choice because it's our hair and not the other person's.

Unlike Ronnie, Kai and Keisha show how external forces help to shape hairstyling practices or choices among black women. Keisha personalizes her account to demonstrate the elusiveness of choice for girls who are rendered powerless at the hands, or "teeth" as it were, of the straightening comb. Kai describes the influence of parents, but potentially the ultimate decision is in the hands of mothers. Although Keisha explains how one's ability to exercise choice is often dependent on age, the issue is still more complex. Ideas about control, as Keisha remarks, continue to inform choice. One's ability to exercise choice may increase with age, but external factors still influence and shape decisions.

Semple approached the issue of choice from the standpoint that external factors, in a sense, prevent one's ability to exercise free will. Agreeing with the women who felt that hair alteration is a sign of self-hatred, Semple argued that the influence of outside forces is often insidious.

SEMPLE: Well I personally am working on the premise that says that our whole existence is a political existence. So there isn't very much that we think, say, or do that doesn't have some type of, at least, political ramifications. And beyond that, social ramifications, and beyond that, sexual ramifications. That can extend into economic, cultural, and all types of things, because of how we [blacks] are here. There are certain things that are just unavoidable. So, in theory one can argue that yes, you can make the decision to wear your hair or cosmetically alter yourself just because you feel that way. In theory, that's a very nice-sounding argument, but in practicality, there are

lots of things that affect and shape you. Even sometimes without you knowing it, your decision about how you present
yourself socially.

Although Semple allows that external forces may be rendered
powerless,[5] it is clear that she places a lot of weight on their
ability to shape black women's perceptions. She challenges Ronnie's argument, which fails to consider external forces. By explaining that utopian ideas about personal choice and free will
are absent when people assess why they do what they do, Semple argues that an individual's actions are never free of external
influences.

To Semple, human existence is always political. If this point is
extended to the feminist statement that the personal is political,
we are faced with two issues that presume the political and personal nature of human existence: (1) If the view that the political
always exists and is dependent on political or other external
forces, then how does the exercising of personal will or choice
come into play? and (2) By defining the personal as political, how
do black women get the ability to exercise choice in shaping their
lives? Although to Semple choice exists within almost completely
external understandings of what is political, her view overlooks
the political in personal power. That is, if every person or act exists on a political level, how can people in general, and black
women in particular, find ways to define and shape various aspects of their lives without external influences? Stacy's comments
below address this issue.

Stacy understands that external forces shape black women's
ability to determine how they wear their hair. Yet unlike Semple,
she sees the possibility for resistance.

STACY: I think there's always influences affecting, and we can't
    not act within the terms of some kind of larger worldview or
    conceptions of ourselves. But I think at the same time it's pos-
    sible to see outside it, especially if you don't embody what
    beauty is in your society. Then it's incumbent upon you to
    figure out another definition that works for you. So yeah, I
    think we make individual lives; pieces with the whole thing
    that are the result of a lot of different influences, not just the

present society that kind of dictates what we're in. But I don't think anybody is ever really that autonomous.

Although Stacy believes that no one is "ever really that autonomous," there is still a notion of choice that surfaces in her implicit reference to black women as not representing the standard of beauty in American society. Stacy addresses choice in relationship to empowerment by explaining that it becomes imperative that black women construct their own notions of beauty. When they do so, they exercise choice. Nevertheless, because several of the women, including Stacy, raised the issue of the influence of external forces, it means that they still continue to play a role in making hairstyling decisions.

Although Andaiye felt that black women have some choice in the way they wear their hair, she viewed choice as being guided by the sign of the times. Although Marcus Garvey rejected the message that black physical characteristics are unattractive by not allowing ads for skin bleachers and hair straighteners in *The Negro World*,[6] it wasn't until the "Black Is Beautiful" generation of the late 1960s that straightened hair would be contested on a large scale. It was the Afro that led the "Black Is Beautiful" cry during that moment in history. Nevertheless, natural styles in general, and the Afro in particular, have also existed and continue to exist within the world of style or fashion. As Andaiye noted, choice is dependent on fashion and fad, which raises questions about external forces influencing black women's decisions.

ANDAIYE: Yeah, definitely. Unfortunately, a lot of the decisions that we make about our lives are in some degree influenced by some type of external decision or what's going on in our communities, you know. Black folks tend to have a thing [for] what the time is calling for. So if it's not what the time is calling for, that's not what we're gettin' ready to do [or] style. Period.

Unlike the others, Andaiye addressed the influence of external forces within the context of style and how black people, follow fads. By placing black women's hairstyling practices, or any other practice of adorning the body, into "what the time is calling for,"

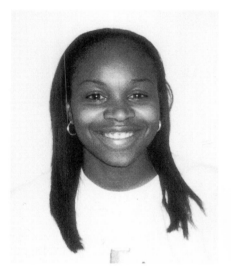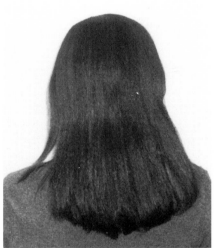

Relaxed/permed

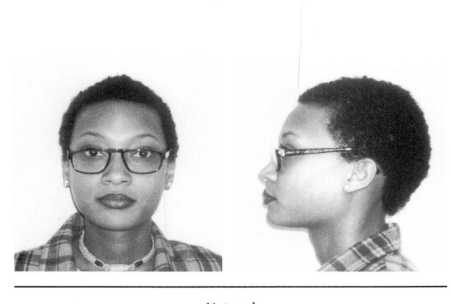

Natural

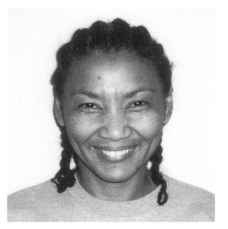 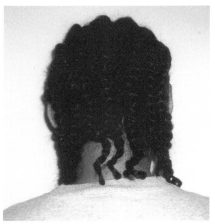

Cornrows

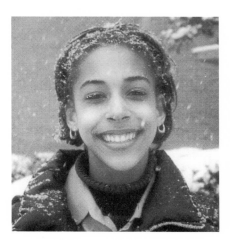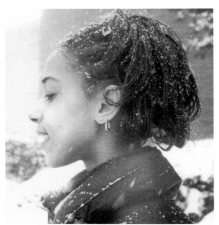

Relaxed/permed

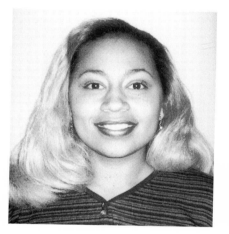 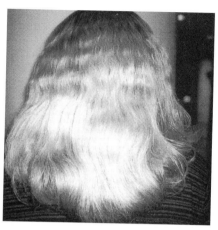

Straight style

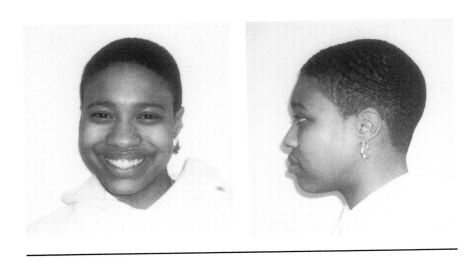

Natural

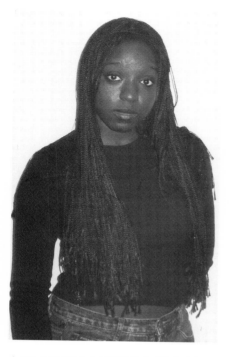

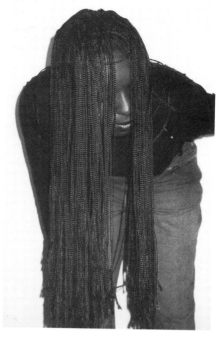

Extensions
(individual braids)

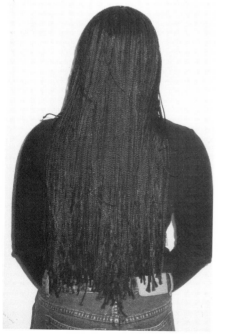

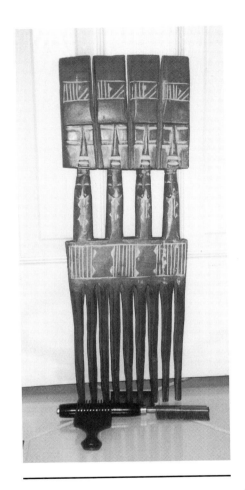

Wood-carved comb (African art piece)
Pressing/straightening comb (floor)
Pick comb (floor)

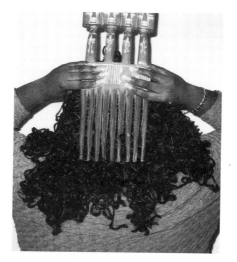

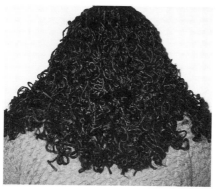

Extensions (crochet braids)

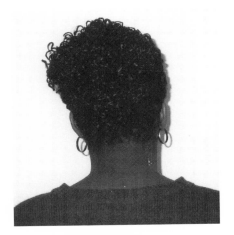

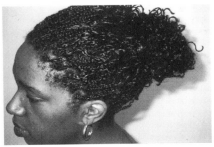

Extension (wavy individual braids)

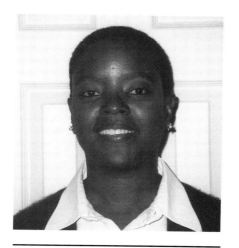

Natural

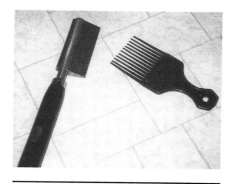

Pressing/straightening comb (left)
and pick comb (right)

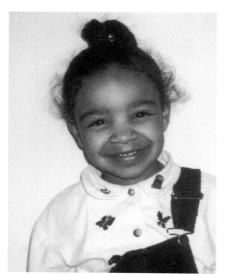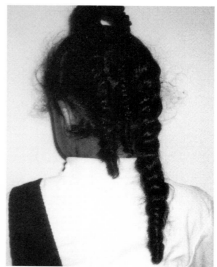

Natural (pigtails)

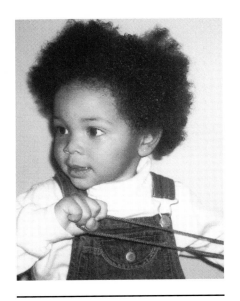

Afro

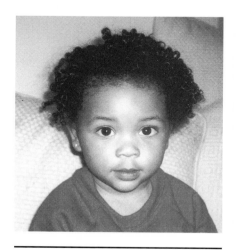

Twists

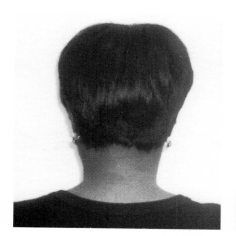 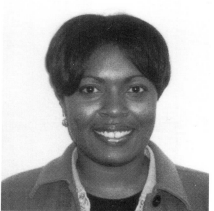

Relaxed/permed

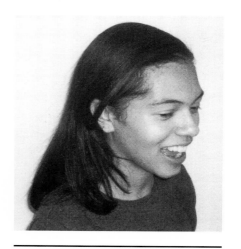

Relaxed/permed

Andaiye illustrates how these practices are not void of external forces. Even if hairstyling practices relate to what's going on in black communities, they still are subject to broader forces that shape black women's ideas about their ability to exercise choice.

Charlene explained what type of woman can exercise the choice to wear her hair natural. She also addressed the question of choice similarly to the question of power earlier in the interview. Again, her comments focus on what it means to be a strong black woman in relationship to external forces.

CHARLENE: We do [have a choice], but you have to be a strong [woman]. And this is funny because I'm contradicting myself. I consider myself to be a strong woman, and at the same time, I feel like you have to be a strong woman to wear your hair naturally when you know it may not be so popular a thing. But you have to look at yourself and know how beautiful you look and go ahead and do it, and then the rest of the world seems to accept you. But then there are those of us, like me, [who] have pressure from home, my mother and my aunts and everybody saying do something to your hair.

In her explanation of how being strong and wearing natural hair is associated with a type of authentic black womanhood, Charlene demonstrates how constructions of gender relate to ideas about hair. Her comments, like others she made during the interview, illustrate how black women who do not go natural, but feel they should, are often ambivalent about their position. Although Charlene sees herself as a strong woman, her ideas about "being strong" are facilitated by what she believes a "true" black woman can endure—the ability to feel beautiful in a community and society where natural hair is "not so popular." As a result, the woman who can pull off such an act will be accepted by others as well as perceived as strong. Still, Charlene's affirmation that she considers herself "strong" *despite* her decision to press her hair is troubling: implicit here is the belief that she is not strong, and by extension, not an "authentic" black woman. What does this mean in relationship to black women's understanding about the definition of womanhood? We will address this question, more specifically in relationship to hair and femininity, in the next section.

On January 3, 1999, hair, in relationship to black women, made primetime again on the ABC weekly one-hour drama *The Practice*. The show is about a group of attorneys in a Boston law firm. In this particular episode, Lucy, the white female receptionist in her early twenties, asks the black female attorney, Rebecca, if she's a lesbian. Rebecca, somewhat puzzled, replies no, but wonders why anyone would assume she is a lesbian. Lucy replies, "With that rump and no guy in your life, and that crop-cut butchy-do hair, [I just assumed you were a lesbian]." Rebecca commences to wonder if the reason she doesn't get asked out is because she "looks butch." Though Rebecca's femininity is marked through her shapely posterior, which is loaded with racialized images of black women's bodies, her hair becomes the ultimate marker of both her womanhood and sexuality. Ideas about the relationship between hair, femininity, and sexuality, as well as images of beauty and male perceptions of femininity, surfaced as the interviewees addressed the question of whether hair is associated with femininity in any way.

Several of the women explained that long hair is associated with femininity and that their beliefs have been nurtured through the mainstream media or other external forces. For example, Pearl explained that she felt sexiest with long hair.

PEARL: Oh I have [associated hair with femininity]. I think the sexiest hairstyle was for me, and this could come from advertisements, television, anywhere, was when my hair was longer and it was piled on top of my head and I would always have little ringlets on the side. And that could also be from my Southern background, and that's how Southern women wore their hair a long time ago. It could stem from my mom. I'm not exactly sure where those images come from but I would look in the mirror and I would see how I look and say, "God, that is sexy, that looks gorgeous."

Pearl associates her perception of long hair with her Southern roots and her mother, but she still questions how she learned what is feminine or sexy. Aria also explained the relationship be-

tween long hair, femininity, and constructions of beauty, but, unlike Pearl, Aria perceived this relationship through gender and
racial readings of hair.

ARIA: Oh please, yes. If I said no I'd be lying because for
years we have been inundated with magazine pictures of
white women and their beautiful bodies and their long,
flowing locks. We have seen commercials, they're [white
women] in the magazine ads. You see them in school flippin'
their hair all through the classroom. I mean I sit in class and
I see these women changing their hairstyles in a fifty-
minute class at least four different times, you know. It's like
come on. We have romance novels that accentuate the long,
silken tresses so there's so many different mediums that por-
tray [long] hair as beautiful, as feminine, as silky. And then
if you have a lack of hair, then your femininity sometimes is
questioned.

Aria points to the white women on television, in magazines, and
in romance novels with long, flowing hair as representative of
femininity in U.S. society. Therefore, femininity is not merely associated with long hair as described by Pearl but with white
women. Aria made a connection to the historical construction of
womanhood, also known as the "cult of the lady" or the "cult of
true womanhood" that represented nineteenth-century U.S. Vic-
torian society (Giddings 1984). Aria's construction of femininity
as exclusive of black women was also true in the cult of true womanhood. Because the cult was based on a socioeconomic class hi-
erarchy[7] and racist and sexist ideologies, there was no place for
black women in the definition of "true" womanhood regardless of
class status.

Aria ends by stating that if a woman lacks hair, her femininity
is questioned. This notion was common among the women. They
associated their understanding of what short hair means in relationship to sexuality and masculinity. Diane explained that an
understanding of what it means to be male and female is embedded in readings of hair length. She also presented a different way
of approaching the image of long, flowing hair among black
women.

DIANE: Oh, yeah. Right or wrong, you'll say stuff like that's a feminine cut, that's not a feminine cut, or whatever. I think to the extent that you have this long, flowing hair that's perceived as very feminine. And the shorter you go, the less feminine it seems to be. So I definitely think that there's some association with that. And the whole interesting thing with the long hair [is] that [it] has some tie back to mainstream culture because not a lot of people in our community have this flowing long hair, but that's defined as being feminine. So when [women] go really short, [people say] that looks too mannish or something. My sister got her hair cut really short one time and she was like, "Oh, now people are going to think that I look like a boy or something."

In Diane's explanation of the relationship between femininity and hair, she presents a scale in which long hair (feminine) and short hair (masculine) exists at the extremes. "Mannish" is associated with "looking like a boy" and long, flowing hair becomes a powerful feminine trait. However, Diane questions placing the image of long, flowing hair among black people, since not many black folk have long, flowing hair. The more telling issue is how black people in general, and black women in particular, understand these meanings, and how ideas that link long hair to femininity are actually acted out. In fact, Indigo explained how her decision to grow dreadlocks has allowed her to fulfill the dream of having long hair.

INDIGO: I think, certainly. I've just begun to take a look at the issue of dreadlocks because I look at myself, and all my life I wanted to have long hair and now I get to have it with dreadlocks. The longer I let it grow I can have this long flowing hair. Of course it won't look like Cheryl Tiegs' hair or, you know, Farah Fawcett's, but it will be my own hair.

Although her observation that white women's hair is the standard of long, flowing hair is similar to Aria's, Indigo sees length as being more important than texture. She displays her perception of femininity through her long hair and, although she recognizes the problem of reinforcing the belief that long hair characterizes femininity, she challenges mainstream standards of beauty through the length of her dreadlocks. Although she doesn't have the same stuff as Tiegs and Fawcett, she does possess the feminine trait, long hair. Thus Indigo's reading of hair permits black women to sit at the table of femininity, despite historical constructions of what constitutes womanhood, and therefore beauty. But the desire to have long hair relates to perceptions of what is considered feminine, and those traits are associated with white women. That is, even with long dreadlocks, the model of long hair, and therefore femininity, are white women like Cheryl Tiegs and Farah Fawcett.

Indigo also explained how shaving her head and having short hair shaped her understanding about hair and femininity. Like other women, she discussed the relationship between sexuality or perceived sexuality with hair, particularly in relationship to lesbianism.

INDIGO: For women, you know, it is a very important part of
   your appearance. Your face, your hair. I mean you can still
   be feminine and have no hair on your head. But you know,
   we have these judgments that only certain women can pull
   that off. I mean actually be bald, and still be considered
   feminine. I know when I shaved off [my hair or the] many
   times I've had my hair short, I was trying to compensate
   with earrings and all this kind of stuff. Trying not to wear
   as many pants because I felt like I was going to be, you
   know, categorized as a dyke, or you know, just deemed
   unattractive.

Cheryl, Jean, Kaliph, and Barbara made similar comments in linking hair to sexuality, as well as to being masculine.

CHERYL: Yeah, I think it is, unfortunately. I cut my hair [short]
   [and] the day I did it I went out to a club with my girl [in the
   nonromantic sense]. It wasn't that crowded, so we were kinda
   hangin' out together and I think we went on the dance floor.
   We weren't even really dancing together but we were, you
   know, dancing without partners and somebody came up to me
   and asked me if like we were together as like a lesbian couple.

Splitting Hairs

And she [my friend] wears dreads. And I was like, it's the hair, isn't it?

JEAN: Oh yeah, definitely. So you know, especially in this town [San Francisco Bay Area] people see a haircut and they say, oh, dyke.

KALIPH: Yes, definitely yes, because, and now I'm thinking in terms of length and lack of length. I hear one of the concerns among my friends who wear their hair short and natural, that there is sometimes a misperception around sexuality like, oh you must be a lesbian if you wear your hair like that. And by definition if you're a lesbian that somehow there's a lack of femininity, you know, you're trying to be a man. You're trying to be male, masculine. So I think there is something about hair, particularly length of hair, that speaks to being feminine and being a woman.

BARBARA: In my view, no. But some men will see a woman with short hair, real short hair, and will think negatively. [Like] a butch cut. I've heard that.

Words such as "butch" and "dyke" describe how ideas about sexuality can be read through hair. Sexual identities are often placed on individuals based on hair, which is why Cheryl concluded that it was her short haircut and her friend's dreadlocks that made others think they were a lesbian couple on the dance floor. Kaliph even shared that she has black female friends with close-cropped and natural hair who are concerned with being perceived as lesbian. Kaliph not only explained that the relationship between hair length is related to sexuality, but also female attractiveness. For example, when Indigo compensated for the lack of hair on her head, she did so by accentuating what she understood as feminine. It is Indigo's concern with being labeled a lesbian and therefore unfeminine that guided her practice of wearing big earrings and more skirts and dresses. In fact, as if in a dialogue with Indigo, Mrs. Franklin supported this reading of hair and femininity.

MRS. FRANKLIN: Yes, I do [think hair is associated with femininity]. Because I like to see women with hair. Most women when they have their hair short, [they] got to get up in the morning [and start] puttin' on make-up, puttin' on earrings and all this kind of stuff so people won't take a second look and say, "Is that a man or a lady?"

Even though Mrs. Franklin appeared to be making a presumption that women with short hair have to highlight their femininity, her thoughts resonate in Indigo's personal account of her insecurities about how her womanhood, in relationship to sexuality, would be read. What Mrs. Franklin and Indigo demonstrate is that black women understand that femininity cannot be reduced to one thing. Although hair is important in black women's understanding of what constitutes femininity, it is not the only marker. However, their comments also contradict their understanding of a more complicated reading of femininity, because if a black woman has long hair, it is not necessary for her to "play up" her femininity by adorning her body in ways that are defined as "feminine." Even if hair is only one of many markers of femininity, or lack thereof, it is definitely one of the most powerful.

In Habiba's reading of the relationship between hair and femininity, she also discussed long hair but used the example of (black) men wearing dreads as indicative of femininity. Femininity is still read through long hair, but Habiba challenged the belief that only women possess feminine characteristics when they have long hair. She also explicitly stated that hair is associated with femininity *and* sexuality.

HABIBA: [Hair is associated with femininity] and sexuality. People oftentimes have their hands in each other's hair, pubic [for example]. So [hair] is very, very sensual. Very, very feminine. And I think men growing the long hair, men with dreads, are also activating that, what is it? They're activating the feminine side. Yes, yes, yes. For men to have the long hair and the dreads. Oh, that's incredible.

Habiba also provided a different view of the sexual nature of hair. Her reading of the relationship between hair and sexuality involves sensuality. Although her discussion supports that long hair is associated with femininity, Habiba's perception of what it means to be masculine is not questioned when she sees black men with long hair. Unlike the explanations of what it means for a woman to wear particularly short hairdos[8] that are perceived as male 'do's, Habiba questioned static notions of gender identities for women and men even as she supported the idea that long hair is associated with femininity. However, Semple's critique of gender readings of hair presents a challenge to how gender is socially constructed. Unlike the other women, Semple discussed this matter within the context of black males and how their hairstyling practices relate to how they are perceived.

SEMPLE: Is hair associated with femininity? I mean, I can see where we've maybe been socialized to think certain hairstyles [are feminine]. [The artist formerly known as] Prince is always thought of as being out the box because he wants to wear a perm and a short cut. Michael Jackson got a little bob cut and people wanted to feminize that whole image. But at the same time, a brother can grow locks down his back and still be seen as extremely masculine. I mean brothers are wearing braids now and people are still [associating certain hairstyles with femininity]. I mean there's an element of "gang society" who walks around with permed hair and curls in their hair.

Unlike Habiba, Semple sees long dreadlocks worn by black men as indicative of masculinity, not femininity. Styles or lengths that are perceived as feminine do not necessarily question the masculinity or sexuality of black men. Semple's discussion of femininity as being read through the hairstyling practices of black men provides a different lens through which to view how black women understand gender through their ideas about hair. Although Semple discusses the hairstyling practices of Michael Jackson and The Artist as influencing their feminization, it is in her discussion of gang culture and the hairstyling practices among younger black males, particularly those in urban areas, which undoubtedly influence and have been influenced by hip-hop culture and rap music, that she contests feminine constructions of hair. Although I am in no way suggesting that rap artist Snoop Dogg is a gangster, his hairstyling practices shed light on Semple's critique. When Snoop appeared on the MTV Music Awards show in New York City a few years ago, his hair was freshly straightened with lots of "Shirley Temple" curls. A year or two later, he was on the same awards show with straightened hair that touched his shoulders. Despite Snoop's hairstyling practices that imitate popular hairstyling practices by (black) women, his "manhood" and sexuality are not called into question. Like other younger black males who are straightening their hair, and wearing braids and cornrows, and barrettes and rubber bands in their hair, Snoop's image is still seen as masculine. In a recent DJ Quik music video, "Youz a Gangsta," Snoop appears with individual braids with beads dangling elegantly at the end of each braid. DJ Quik's hairstyle changes from cornrows to a straightened style by the end of the video. In another recent video, "Thug Mentality," rap artist Krayzie Bone appears with beautiful cornrows, and one of his posse members stands by his side with the same type of braided and beaded style as Snoop in DJ Quik's video. The video represents the life of a thug, with car chases and gambling rounding out the message of the video. Despite their hairdos, in both of these videos, the main characters' masculinity and sexuality are never questioned because they are gangstas and thugs. This was true in the 1970s, as well, within the urban pimp-culture scene. No one challenged Ron O'Neal's masculinity in the blaxploitation film, *Super Fly*. If anything, he was hypermasculinized and seen as the perfect example of a "brother's brother," that is, a man's man. He had women, money, sharp clothes, a nice apartment, and a fancy car. And he had straightened ("fly") hair.

What Semple's observation suggests is that gender identity is not static. But given the comments by other women who addressed the relationship between hair and femininity, a nonstatic reading, or even a cross-reading, of gender does not occur when women's hairstyling practices resemble those that are considered masculine. Whereas all black men are not labeled as feminine or gay when they sport hairdos that are generally perceived as feminine, when black women wear their hair close-cropped they are constructed as being unfeminine, unattractive, masculine, and lesbian.

As Indigo's and Mrs. Franklin's comments demonstrate, women have to play up their femininity in other ways. Though some black men such as The Artist and Michael Jackson are constructed as feminine, this labeling is also due to other characteristics.[9] The Superfly types and Snoop Dog may wear the same hairstyle as The Artist and Michael Jackson, but their manhood is not questioned because their other characteristics speak to a particular type of black masculinity. This point is even clearer in Semple's association with black male (as well as Latino and Chicano) gang culture. These boys and men sport cornrows and braids with barrettes and rubberbands, hairstyles traditionally worn by black girls and women. However they are never perceived as feminine or gay, whereas Indigo explained that it was her lack of hair that made her feel less feminine, and Cheryl explained that her short hairdo marked her as a lesbian.

There is a tradition of black men straightening their hair that can be traced back to the early twentieth century (Craig 1997; White and White 1998), hence there is a history of black women and men practicing similar hairstyling methods. However, as Craig argues in her discussion of the consciousness-raising period of the 1960s, it is imperative to understand the difference that gender made in assessing how the same hairstyles worn by black women and men were read differently.

> Though in the rhetoric of black consciousness men and women were encouraged with equal fervor to wear naturals, straightening hair had different meanings and different chronologies for Black men and Black women. These differences were masked beneath a discourse of racial unity that ignored the specifically gendered ways racial domination expressed itself in the lives of men and women. (p. 404)

I argue that within a 1990s context, the hairstyling practices that cross gender boundaries for men go unchallenged, while those for black women (i.e., a buzz cut) do not; this is because people living in a sexist and homophobic society receive certain messages about what constitutes gender identity and sexuality. The hairstyles of black male basketball stars Allen Iverson and Latrell Sprewell, as they are characterized in the media, actually *add* to their depiction of being hyper-masculine. A gender reading indeed, but here masculinity is increased, whereas when women don buzz cuts, their femininity is decreased.

The topic of black men arose in other areas as well. Some of the women addressed men's perceptions of women's hair and how they help shape women's beliefs about femininity. These comments reflect the investment that women see men as having in upholding feminine virtue through women's hairstyling practices. Ebony discussed her father's preoccupation with long hair whereas Asara retold a conversation she had with a male neighbor.

EBONY: Oh, my gosh, so most definitely is it. That's where my family aspect comes into it. My father, for him, a woman is someone who has long hair. And so every time I'm like, "Well, Dad, you know I think I'm going to cut my hair," he says, "Please, no! Don't cut your hair! Tell me before you cut your hair so I can convince you not to!" He's offered me incentives not to cut my hair. "I'll get you this, I'll get you that, I'll take you to the beauty salon." So for him, that's what being a woman is, someone with long hair.

ASARA: Men think it is. I had this neighbor tell me that when I wore my hair long and pressed that I looked like a little girl and I was so pretty to him. I *was* so pretty to him. But when I got my hair cut and started wearing it short, it made me look like a boy. So I said to him, "So I'm not pretty to you anymore?" [He stated], "Well, you were prettier when you wore your hair long and styled."

Even when black women resist associating long hair with femininity, they recognize black men's ideas about images of beauty and their investment in these images. But there are also black women who buy into this belief. This was evident in Kai's statement.

KAI: Yeah, I think so in a way 'cause you tend to wanna look your best for it to be perceived by males as looking nice so you want your whole person to be beautiful and your hair is a part of that. So you would want to be, I guess what's considered desirable, which is usually just long straight hair.

Like Kai, other teens that I interviewed during a focus-group session discussed external influences on hairstyling practices. This issue, along with several others, emerged during the five focus group sessions that frame the next chapter.

chapter 4

Women and Girls Speak Out
Five Hair-Raising Sessions

There's always a question of race, money, and sex. But I think for black women, it's race, money, sex, and hair. It transcends a cosmetic [or esthetic] issue because it is at the base historically, culturally, and politically.

Wixie

That was my college essay, my life changed after my first haircut, that's how the essay started. It was all about hair and how that it was a symbol for lots of stuff.

Adrianna

Hair is one of the most talked about subjects among black women. Focus group research can be viewed as a way of re-creating these casual discussions. Moreover, talking to groups of women also brings a different dimension to the data collected in individual interviews. Below, I present specific comments and conversations from the focus group sessions I held, as well as discuss the dynamics of each session in greater detail.

The decision to conduct focus groups with groups of girls and women who are friends proved to be fruitful for several reasons. First, a breaking-the-ice period was unnecessary because everyone knew everyone else. The discussions that follow demonstrate that the girls and women were very comfortable among each other discussing how hair shapes black women's ideas about a host of issues. Given that friends are usually similar in terms of age, occupation, educational status, and so on, the respective focus groups were fairly homogeneous in membership.[1]

The focus groups were as follows: the Teen Group, the Early Twenty-Something Group, the Graduate Student Group, the

Physicians Group, and the Low-Income Group. In this chapter we will discuss issues that emerged in each session but did not necessarily arise in the individual interviews, even though some did. For example, the girls and women were asked all or most of the questions that were also asked in the individual interviews, but because of the group atmosphere other issues arose. The goal was to let the focus groups evolve naturally; my only intervention was to present another question or issue, or to ask for a clarification of statements. This allowed for a more free-flowing dialogue that resembles real-world discussions among black women.

The Teen Group

This was the smallest "group," but the two girls, Tatiana and Latrice, who are neighbors and close friends, made up in discussions what they lacked in numbers. Tatiana is a fifteen-year-old high school sophomore who lives in Los Angeles. She has very long hair, and depending on which strand you look at, it is at once straight, wavy, and curly. Both of Tatiana's parents are physicians[2] and she has a younger sister and a half-brother. Latrice is also a fifteen-year-old high school sophomore who was born and raised in Los Angeles. Latrice's hair is long and it is naturally straight and wavy, depending, once again, on which part of her hair one considers. Her mother is a ticket agent for an airline carrier, her dad works in security, and she has two brothers and two sisters. Within the context of U.S. black communities, Tatiana and Latrice have what is considered "good hair."

I had initially come to Tatiana's house to talk with a group of black women physicians whom Tatiana's mother had brought together, as well as to conduct individual interviews with Tatiana and her younger sister, Elisa. After I had interviewed Elisa alone and the three women physicians together, Tatiana's mother suggested I also try to talk to some of Tatiana's other friends. I approached Tatiana about a focus group session with some of her friends, and she immediately went to the phone to try to gather up friends in the neighborhood who were at home on a very warm Sunday afternoon. The only friend home that afternoon was Latrice. Latrice came over immediately and I told her about the study. She was very receptive and ran home to obtain parental consent. She came back with the consent form signed, and we began the session. We sat on couches in a very comfortable and large nook that adjoined a big, bright modern kitchen in Tatiana's home.

External Influences on Hairstyling Practices

It was clear that Tatiana and Latrice were close friends and felt comfortable engaging each other. It was also clear that they really enjoyed the engagement and interaction, as well as reflecting on issues that were funny, controversial, and personal in nature. It was immediately evident that these girls are bright and had opinions about the forces that shape their lives. Both girls felt that hair matters among black girls and women. Although they discussed the choice of hairstyling practices as an individual choice to a certain extent, both agreed that external factors such as boys, friends, and parents shape these practices, particularly with regard to teens.

Both girls discussed the control that parents have on the hairstyling practices of black girls. Tatiana explained that economic factors shape this influence.

TATIANA: And also the choice because your mama has to pay for the hair, so she is an important factor because we as black young women do not have jobs. So her money, basically, is very important because if she doesn't like it, you're not getting it, you know what I'm sayin'.

Ideas about choice are predicated on economic factors, a reality Tatiana sees as interfering with teen girls' ability to make autonomous choices about their hair. Latrice agreed with Tatiana but provided a personal example of how a parent's economic influence has the *potential* to influence how girls wear their hair.

LATRICE: Or my dad, he doesn't like my hair curly at all. He likes it when it's straight, when it's blow-dried and stuff. He went so far as [to say], "I'll pay for you to get a haircut if you don't [wear it curly]." He'd rather me wear it short if I want to wear it curly and I don't want to cut my hair.

Unlike Ebony's father, whose preference revealed men's investment in long hair, Latrice's dad is invested in straight hair. In a followup comment after a probing question, Latrice revealed that she did not take the bait that her father presented, showing that she had the ability to exercise a choice, which Tatiana did not believe black girls have because they are subject to the whims of "Mom's pocketbook."

The above comments notwithstanding, neither girl saw the economic clout of parents or parental opinion as being a major influence on their hairstyling practices. Tatiana and Latrice began an interesting exchange that involved the influence that peers have on their hairstyling practices. Whereas Tatiana stressed the importance of friends in particular, Latrice responded to Tatiana's comments by discussing a broader societal context.

TATIANA: But I think it's more of the friends who have a bigger impact on you because they'll say something. I know if they don't think that a style is cute, they won't say bluntly, but basically, you'll rarely wear that hairstyle again just because they said it. And you might think it's the best hairstyle you've ever seen in your life.

LATRICE (responds): Overall, that's society because where do your friends get the idea that it's not cute, you know? A lot of people [will] tell [you], "I haven't seen anyone wear that style, that's not cute." But then it's like, you'll say, my friend didn't like it, so I won't wear it like that. And then you go out and you're like, wait a minute, that's the style I just wore last week and you see like five people wearing it. So you're like oh forget it, you know, I'm going to wear it like that. And you tell your friends you saw like ten people wear it. So it's like a lot of different people have impact, so sometimes your friends get overruled by different people that you see.

This exchange is an example of the kind of conversational atmosphere that occurred during the focus group sessions. On another level it demonstrates the complex and often contradictory nature of articulations about choice and hairstyling practices that were evident in the individual interviews as well. For example, although Latrice made a very perceptive point in reaction to Tatiana's comments by stating that beliefs of peer groups are shaped by the larger society and how friends are, as she says, "overruled" by people outside of peer group networks, her comments still simultaneously support and deny choice. On the one hand, when teens decide to wear a particular style because they see people outside of their peer group wearing it, despite the group's disapproval, there is a sense of empowerment in their decision. However, the whims of peer group pressure do not govern choice per se. Instead, approval or acceptance may be based on what's considered stylish within the fashion world, for example.

Ideas about "choice" present conflicting issues once again. Nevertheless, Latrice showed a keen sense of analysis by actually challenging the governance that teen peer group networks have over individuals. No doubt some of the most daunting networks that individuals experience in life exist among kids and adolescents. Therefore, although Latrice demonstrated how external factors can influence girls' hairstyling practices, she nevertheless challenged the notion of the all-mighty or powerful influence that peer group networks have over teenagers.

"Good Hair" and Mate Choices

One of the most interesting discussions that surfaced during the discussion with Tatiana and Latrice involved "good hair" and mate choices. Before sharing the comments by Tatiana and Latrice, I should add that at this point in the discussion Tatiana's younger sister, Elisa, whom I had interviewed earlier, came downstairs so I invited her to sit in as well. I didn't want her to feel that she was not privy to the discussion with her sister and Latrice, and everyone was comfortable with her sitting in. In fact, she stated that she just wanted to sit and listen. However, Elisa did join the discussion when Tatiana brought up the subject about "good hair" and mate choices.

Tatiana began by stating that she was aware of the political incorrectness of what she was about to share, but she was going to say it anyway. I was happy, to say the least, that she felt comfortable verbalizing her feelings about what I think we all felt was a very sensitive and controversial matter. Instead of interrupting the flow of this discussion by inserting my comments after each statement, I present the heart of the discussion below in its entirety.

TATIANA: I just admitted this to one of my friends . . . we were washing dishes like a long time ago and we just admitted we were thinking about when we get older what kind of man we are going to look for, and the hair came up because that's important. I know I'm happy I have this kind of hair and I couldn't imagine myself going to the beauty shop every other week to get this mess conked out. [Since] I've had this hair all my life I couldn't see myself paying to get it done every two weeks, but if I had to do it, I'd do it. But we just like admitted secretly that we wanted to marry a guy with the same kind of hair that we have . . . the kind of hair texture as mine because I want my child, and I'm not saying that it's a disadvantage . . .

ELISA (interrupts): I want my child's hair to be curly personally. There's nothing wrong with other types of hair, but it seems easier . . .

INGRID: What do you mean by curly? Like yours, or?

ELISA: No. Like theirs (Tatiana and Latrice). Curly, where you can wet it. But you have the best of both worlds because you can have it curly one day or if you don't feel like doing your kids hair then you can blow dry it one day and have it nice and flowing.

LATRICE: My mom told me that your hair changes texture, not drastically, but in little ways.

TATIANA (continues): But I was just saying that I want to have a husband that will ensure that my kid [will have my kind of hair]. I want her to have it as easy as it seems that I have in comparison to like my other friends who have natural [black hair] because they always talk about how easy it seems my hair is, so I want my child to be able to, you know what I'm

Women and Girls Speak Out

sayin', roll in the shower and have the ability to go swimming or whatever, just kind of jump in the pool rather than puttin' on swim caps. I know a lot of my friends who have natural or typical black hair that you might think of, they always talk about how I have good hair.

LATRICE (interrupts): There's a good chance that your child can come out with hair like yours but there's a chance they won't. I mean, you can have a family member from 1780 who had kinky hair and your kid will get it. I'm serious, just like eyes and [other] features, your hair can skip whole generations. Just like a friend of mine. She's really light but her dad is dark but she came out really light and the same thing with the hair. I would really like to have my kid have the same kind of hair as I do and marrying somebody with my type of hair may give it a better chance, but you just still have to know that there's a chance that they may not have that kind of hair.

TATIANA: I still want my child [to have my hair]. I mean I'm not going to marry a wife beater just because he has really nice long hair. If I fall in love with a guy who is like, you know, then I'll be like, things happen. Maybe it's God's nature or whatever. But if I can help it, you know what I'm saying, I'm most likely going to if it's someone to marry or to mate. If I'm dating someone, [hair texture] doesn't matter. If he treats me well and I think he's cute and I'm hearing Marvin Gaye or whatever, then I'm going to be with him and get married and stuff, but basically [I'll be looking to marry someone with "good hair"].

This exchange demonstrates the utility of conducting focus groups among friends as a way to gain an understanding of why hair matters so much among black women. I would argue that if Tatiana was in a focus group in which she had just met the participants, I don't think she would have been willing to initiate this aspect of our conversation, which is why focus group sessions, at least those investigating personal issues, are better utilized among close friends.

Obviously the most striking point in this exchange is that hair would be a factor in Tatiana's mate choices when she gets older.

People make choices about partners based on physical character-istics every day, so her position is not a stretch of the imagination. Furthermore, Tatiana noted that if she falls in love with a man who does not have hair like hers, then the relationship was meant to be.

In response to Tatiana, Latrice explained how Tatiana's wishes for the "good" tresses of her future offspring may not come true. Latrice's point demonstrates how personal desire that is often nurtured by social and cultural beliefs has the potential of being denied by biological processes. In addition, Latrice explained the different biological makeup of U.S. blacks that has been shaped by historical and personal intra- and interracial unions, and how these unions determine genetics across generations. As a result Tatiana's plans may be stifled even if she marries a man with hair texture that is similar to hers.

However, what is most telling about Tatiana's comment is that it's not that "good hair" is more attractive in terms of es-thetics because, after all, hair texture does not matter with guys she only dates. It is the "attractiveness" of "good hair" on the level of grooming practices that is central to her desire, as she noted, to "ensure" that her children, particularly any daughters, will be blessed with "good hair." Tatiana's position is reinforced by her friends who have tightly coiled black hair, as well as by her sister Elisa who, although she has long and beautiful hair, does not have her sister's texture. This is a point that emerged in the individual interviews, too, and illustrates how understandings about hair among black girls and women are often based on what the individual has in comparison to others. In all three girls comments, it's not just about texture or, in a broader sense, about hair, but a type of lifestyle that their children, particularly girls, will be able to have. For example, Elisa discussed the choices that girls and their parents, or guardians for that matter, have with regard to grooming prac-tices; she wants to have kids with hair texture like Tatiana's and Latrice's. Choice is not just about grooming practices but a sense of freedom that lurks under ideas about "good hair," as seen in the following exchange between Tatiana and Latrice.

LATRICE: And during the summer you can swim endlessly.

TATIANA: Yeah, I can go swimming without a swim cap or I can
just walk in the rain. I can go months without having my hair
done, you know what I'm saying. I just get my hair done
when I feel I want a straight look, but it's not mandatory
when I have to go. But because of that, people always say,
mostly girls, other teenagers, [that I have good hair and therefore I don't have to do anything with it].

In earlier comments about "good hair" Tatiana attempted to challenge the notion of "good hair" by noting her position after others state that she doesn't have to do anything to her hair because
of its texture. The following is a synopsis of Tatiana's responses to
this issue:

TATIANA: I mean, what's good hair? I have to comb [it] out. I
just kinda get mad at these people who say "you got that good
hair. . . . You probably don't do anything to it." Or when I
have it straight, because most girls rap their hair, but personally, I just go to sleep and wake up. Sometimes I bump the
ends, and they're like the next morning, "Oh, you wrapped
your hair?" And I say "No, I just went to sleep." And they
say, "Oh, I forgot, you have that good hair," or something like
that. And I'm thinking, "Good?" I swear I had to comb this
out this morning. If it was so good . . . I mean I guess there are
different levels of good, but to me, I mean, yes, I notice the
advantages of having this kind of hair because I don't have to
go every two weeks to get it conked out [straightened] or
whatever.

Even within Tatiana's challenge of what is "good hair" she still
understands the "advantages" on the level of grooming practices
that she has in comparison to black girls and women who have
tightly coiled black hair. Tatiana says it is easier to groom her hair
because she knows that girls and women with a different kind of
texture have a harder time. Although she has to comb her hair she
sees her own ritual of combing as less taxing than that of women
with a tightly coiled texture.

Finally, although the idea of "good hair" was implicit in the
earlier exchange between Tatiana, Latrice, and Elisa, they did not

use the term "good." When Tatiana and Latrice used it in other responses they were quoting others who felt that they had "good hair." This shows that, although black girls place a value on straight hair texture, it is not a value that is good or bad to them in terms of attractiveness. The Early Twenty-Something focus group raised similar issues.

The Early Twenty-Something Group

The topics discussed in the Early Twenty-Something Group were just as discerning as those in the Teen Group. Four friends who had grown up together participated. Crystallina, who is twenty-one, was born and raised in Los Angeles. She has a B.A. in Women's Studies and is currently an elementary-school teacher in South Central Los Angeles. She has long shoulder length hair and wears it natural. Mercedes was born in Brooklyn but was raised in Los Angeles. She is twenty-two, an undergraduate, and a receptionist. She has long, shoulder-length hair and straightens it with a pressing comb. Patricia, twenty-two, was born in Washington, D.C., but raised in Los Angeles. She has a B.S. in chemistry and is currently a physician's assistant and plans to enter medical school in the fall (1997). She has long hair, halfway down her back, and wears it natural. Shaquanda, a twenty-four-year old with a B.A. in theater arts was born in Washington, D.C., but was raised in Los Angeles. She is currently an unemployed actress, and wears her hair long, halfway down her back, and relaxed in a straight and wavy style.

The session took place at Crystallina's parents house in Los Angeles.[3] I arrived before the other three young women, so I sat down with Crystallina and her older brother for a minute to chat. Minutes later Shaquanda and Mercedes arrived, and I began to give them some background about my research. As I began collecting demographic data from them, Patricia arrived. After the consent forms were signed and the demographic data were collected, we went to the exercise room in the house to begin the session. It was just the right size. We sat in a circle on the carpeted floor and began discussing why hair matters.

Crystallina and Mercedes discussed the importance of hair and its relationship to adornment practices and appearance and also felt that although hair is an issue among black women, it really doesn't have to be. Shaquanda and Patricia were a bit more expressive about the significance of hair. For example, although Shaquanda felt on a personal level that hair is, as she stated, "unimportant," she did understand the importance it carries within a broader societal context.

SHAQUANDA: I think hair is so unimportant. I think hair is so unimportant. I think it's important to people who make it important, who are like, "Oh my God, I have to fit into this certain style, and oh my God, people aren't going to think I'm cute." Whatever. They're being sucked into what society says is pretty or not pretty, or cool or not cool. I think hair is so stupid. And maybe that's because I don't do my hair. Yeah, if I could I would chop it off but I think my face is too fat to do that.

Although Shaquanda was adamant in her position that hair is "unimportant" and "stupid," she did allow that it's important enough, at least for the sake of appearance, not to cut hers off because of the shape of her face.[4] Therefore, her criticism of people who make it important is problematic because despite her comments, it is of importance to her as well. The contradiction that was evident in Shaquanda's comments also surfaced in Patricia's. Similar to Shaquanda, Patricia discussed the importance of hair for black people and used her personal experience to illustrate her point.

PATRICIA: I don't think about hair too much. My sisters used to get on me, you know what I mean, because they have like a little bit curlier hair, you know. So like, they'd get on me about it but I wouldn't even be stressed about [it]. I find that other black people have something, you know what I'm saying, against you if you have this type of hair and that type of hair. I think it's very important to black people. The texture, and people marry people with certain types of hair. It's really superficial, shallow. I don't, you know, feed into it as much as people would think I do [because of] the type of hair that I have.

Although Patricia noted that she does not think about hair too much, there is still an understanding that she has thought about it enough to understand what it means to have her type of hair vis-à-vis that of her sisters. Similar to the earlier discussion by the Teen Group, she pointed out the relationship between hair and marriage partners and commented on the shallow nature of choosing a lifelong partner based on hair textufre. Patricia, like Tatiana and Latrice, has "good hair." Her own understanding that she has "good hair" is clear when she noted that her sisters have hair that is a bit curlier,[5] but that she doesn't feed into the superficiality of hair "as much as people might think" despite her hair texture. Patricia also gave the impression that the reason she feels that hair matters is because of the significance that others place on *her hair*. It became clear that she has been so bludgeoned with comments about her hair that she would rather not deal with it or even discuss it. In fact, her question as to what I was trying to prove by conducting such a study had less to do with questioning my research project than with her desire to "forget" about the attention her hair receives.[6] In addition, although Patricia and Shaquanda claim that they don't think about hair too much and that hair is unimportant, both are speaking from the vantage point of black women with hair that is admired in black communities and the broader U.S. society. When speaking from a privileged position, it is hard for individuals to see an advantage, which was an issue that surfaced as the discussion continued.

The points made by all the women, including the comments by Crystallina and Mercedes that I summarized, are significant because they set the stage for one of the most provocative discussions that emerged during the session. The fact that these women were friends and therefore felt comfortable in confronting one another was key. It was clear that they always engaged each other in heated discussions in their tight-knit friendship circle. There is no better way to demonstrate this than to present part of the discussion here. It begins when Shaquanda brings up the issue of "good hair" without being prompted by anyone.

"Good Hair" Again

SHAQUANDA: I want to respond to this good-hair, bad-hair thing. I hate that more than anything. I hate the "good hair." What the hell is good hair? If you get up and comb your hair and it looks cute in the morning, that's good hair as far as I'm concerned regardless of what texture it is or what color it is or whatever. There's some girls that had their hair looking slick [when I was in college]; short little Afros, short little like twists and it looked dope. To me, that was good hair, do you know what I mean? But the problem that I would get saying all these things is that, "Well, look at your hair . . . you don't have a right to say this isn't an issue if your hair, if you don't worry about your hair, if your hair isn't [tightly coiled]. But I do have a right because, I think, because I have the hair that I have I think I can say that it's stupid, get over it.

INGRID: Anybody else want to speak on the good/bad hair issue?

MERCEDES: I think that because it's '96 and because it's not necessarily fashionable to be so color struck and to be so, like, you know, "Oh my God, I want a light-skin girl with long hair," people have taken or assumed a role like there isn't good hair and bad hair when there [is]. And it's "pretty" hair now, it's not good hair, it's "pretty hair." It's just like they don't want to be so outward with it whereas back in the '80s when we were all in the seventh and eighth grade you wanted a boyfriend that was light-skinned and no darker than a paper bag, and when the wind blew, his hair should move. And that was okay to say. So it's a lot of contradictions going on. I think that because of the time and the climate it's not necessarily sociable to admit that you really don't understand or you haven't been talked through or led out of the whole concept of having good hair, having bad hair, you know what I'm saying? Within our own realm we are continually perpetuating the same kind of shit that we're trying to get ourselves out of.

INGRID: We're talking about the good versus bad hair issue. Patricia, do you want to make a comment?

CRYSTALLINA: Patricia, you're not very talkative today. Come on, Pat!

PATRICIA: Good hair, bad hair, whatever, it's hair.

SHAQUANDA: But you've had that experience, right?

PATRICIA: I don't listen to people when they say crap about hair because it's just so stupid to me. You know, "What do you have? Are you mixed?"

CRYSTALLINA: But the bottom line is that shit still exists.

PATRICIA: I don't deny that it exists. I don't pay attention to it. I really don't. It goes in one ear and out the other.

CRYSTALLINA: What if you had nappy-ass hair?

SHAQUANDA: See, I wasn't going to say that. I was going to say that the reason we don't care is because of society. We would get pounced on if we did.

CRYSTALLINA: If y'all had some nappy-ass hair, hair would be an issue, period.

INGRID: Why do you say that, Crystallina?

CRYSTALLINA: For example, if Shaquanda had nappy hair it would be an issue because she would get no jobs.

SHAQUANDA: That's not true. I'd be up for different roles. See, you have to understand that I would . . .

CRYSTALLINA (interrupts): There aren't that many different roles.

SHAQUANDA: Yes, there are.

CRYSTALLINA: No, there aren't.

MERCEDES: There are different roles that she'd be called up for because her hair is like that.

SHAQUANDA: I get called for the hooker. I get called for the stripper. No, I don't really get called for the stripper—that's just this one-time thing that was just a surprise. I get called for like the ditzie girlfriend. It's like the blonde thing. Isn't it, Mercedes?

MERCEDES: Yes

SHAQUANDA: It's like being a black blonde white woman.

MERCEDES: We are the blondes of the black culture, there you go.

SHAQUANDA: That totally is so right. God, man, that was so right.

MERCEDES: And, just for the record, I think I can be safe in
saying, because I've known all you guys pretty much all my
life. If we had to just go there and do a nappy scale, my hair
is nappy, you know what I'm saying, in comparison to
[yours].

SHAQUANDA: But it's not, it's not!

CRYSTALLINA: Wait, I have something to say because Mercedes
said that hair would not be an issue if Shaquanda and Patricia
had nappy-ass hair.

MERCEDES: That's not what I said, that's what y'all said, I
didn't say that. I said not necessarily.

CRYSTALLINA: No, I said that hair would be an issue.

MERCEDES: I said not necessarily.

CRYSTALLINA (pointing as she talked): I think hair would be an
issue for you (Patricia), you (Shaquanda), and for me if we had
some nappy-ass hair. Period. That's just what I think.

INGRID: Why do you think that's the case? I think that's a very
provocative statement, but why do you think that's the case?

CRYSTALLINA: Well, for me, I know I wouldn't know what the
hell to do with my hair. You know what I mean?

SHAQUANDA: Your whole life would have been different then.

GROUP: Yes, yes.

CRYSTALLINA: For example, I was raised with Mercedes and I
know that hair was an issue for Mercedes when we were
growing up. You know what I'm saying? She knew what kind
of hair she [had] when she was born. I grew up with Mercedes
and I just know hair was an issue. Plus, all of us went to
white schools, and hair would have been an issue. I saw Robin
and Toni and all the people we went to school with who had
nappy hair and . . .

SHAQUANDA (interrupts): But it wasn't an issue for me.

CRYSTALLINA (interrupts and continues): Quiet. And hair was
an issue for them. I remember white girls coming up to Robin
and asking her why her hair didn't blow in the wind? Why
her hair didn't grow?

INGRID: Were they asking you the same questions?

CRYSTALLINA: No. They would say, "Robin, why doesn't your
hair blow in the wind?"

INGRID: And Robin has tightly coiled hair?

CRYSTALLINA: She has some shit [nappy hair]. They would say, "How come your hair does not grow?" I'm serious, all of them, everyone. Even the white girls who were like down with the black people would still ask those stupid-ass questions.

SHAQUANDA: That's because they were ignorant.

CRYSTALLINA: But the bottom line is hair was an issue for all of them [the girls with nappy hair] and it would have been an issue for all us. Period. Hair was an issue for me even with my shit [good hair], you know what I'm saying?

Two of the most important moments in the comments above were when Crystallina challenged Patricia and Shaquanda on their stance about why hair matters and when Mercedes stated that compared to her three friends, she has nappy hair. First, Crystallina's challenge. Crystallina understands and reinforces the perceived privilege that comes with "good hair." For example, when I asked Crystallina why she thinks hair would be an issue for her, Shaquanda, and Patricia if they all had "nappy-ass hair," she responded that she would not know what to do with her hair, a point which was also raised among the teens. For black women to understand what to do with tightly coiled black hair, they not only have to be born with it, but they must learn how to groom it. Crystallina assumes that she would never learn how to do her hair if it were like Robin's, not because of what she knows personally, but because of what she understands about "good hair" and "bad hair." Crystallina also views having "good hair" as having more to do with hair manageability than with privilege per se, a comment that was evident in the individual interviews and during the teen session. Although ideas about "good hair" may appear to be predicated on being more attractive and therefore desirable, most of the girls and women in the individual and group interviews explained that the desirable trait is manageability, which "good hair" allows. Although these ideas are also loaded with social and cultural baggage, it was interesting to me that ideas about what is more or less esthetically pleasing are absent in these discussions. Still, within a broader social context and political correctness, Mercedes explained how comments about "pretty" hair are indeed rearticulations of what black people refer to as "good hair." In this sense, the ideas about nappy hair that were voiced among the adults protesting against Carolivia Herron's *Nappy Hair* have not changed. Although the words may change, they are only coded and provide evidence that an understanding of what is "bad hair" and "good hair" continues to exist.

It is interesting that the privilege that their "good hair" affords them is never addressed directly by Shaquanda and Patricia. Although Shaquanda does make an attempt to address the question when she said that she would be up for different roles if she had "nappy" hair, she did not directly address Crystallina's question. Because they were silent on this particular issue but very vocal and detailed during other parts of the session, it could be that Crystallina touched on an issue that made these young women uncomfortable. By addressing the question, they would have had to deal with something that they may have never considered: what it would be like to be the "other."

The Graduate Student Group

The Graduate Student Group also consisted of four friends, three of whom were in the same graduate program. Terri arranged the focus group and is thirty. She is a second-year graduate student who was raised in Danville, California. She lives in Oakland, California, and wears her hair in a close-cropped, natural style. Eve, age twenty-seven, is also a second-year graduate student and was raised in Oakland. She wears her hair in long braids with extensions. Adrianna is a twenty-five-year-old, second-year graduate student who was born and raised in San Francisco where she still lives. She wears her hair long and naturally wavy. Allison is a twenty-eight-year-old college graduate with a degree in communicative disorders. She is an urban project development manager. Like Terri, she wears her hair close-cropped and natural.

The focus group took place at Terri's house in Oakland on a Friday evening. When I arrived, Adrianna and Eve were already there and Allison arrived a little while thereafter. The atmosphere was very relaxing, and we sat on couches in the living room arranged in an L-shaped design.

The women spoke candidly about hair on a personal level. One question I asked was how old they were when they began noticing that there was something to hair. Amazingly, three of the four women placed these origins at four or five years old. What is striking is the age at which such a recognition occurred, and how such recognition was played out by these women. For example, Terri made the following comment.

TERRI: Holidays. That was the time when I had my hair pressed. It was Christmas, Easter, and we would wear Shirley Temple rings and you would be able to fling it around and squish and the whole bit with your head and play little white girl kind of hair. And when we didn't have our hair pressed or out like that we would wear the T-shirt on our head, you know, to make your hair long and flowing. And we even had headbands and the whole bit to go with the T-shirt. So yeah, that was a very young age, maybe four, five, when you start to pretend about hair, and I think that's probably the age you start really noticing the difference. And the Barbie dolls that we got did not have curly hair. They had long straight blonde hair that we would comb and braid and try to do like our hair. So we would do the same to the doll.

Terri's description of "playing white girl kind of hair," playing with T-shirts and headbands, and braiding Barbie's hair demonstrates why it isn't surprising that, at the age of four or five, she already knew about the importance of hair. Kids play, and during moments of play, in this particular instance, Terri acted out what she saw, through images,[7] as the type of hair that was deemed beautiful and desirable. This is an important point in understanding how socialization shapes children even before they enter grade school. It became clear that cultural understandings influenced Terri's play as well. By braiding and cornrowing Barbie's hair, black hairstyling practices emerged despite mainstream notions of beautiful hair. Even in those moments of play, cultural practices were not made invisible.

Eve also recalled similar early personal experiences about hair. Her response was a bit more explicit and inclusive of the forces

that shape young girls' perceptions about what and who is considered beautiful.

EVE: I think probably about four. Yeah, I was in kindergarten, so it was four. And just noticing the attention that this girl named Tracy was getting. Big ponytails, long hair. And that was pretty, you know, at the time. So you realize that's pretty, that's not me, so therefore I'm not [pretty]. And you get the messages from your family and everywhere. And from dolls.

Similar to comments in the other focus groups and individual interviews, Eve's perception of her position on the ladder of beauty was based not on her physical attributes per se, but on those of girls like Tracy. There is also an implicit notion here that Eve received messages from her family, or particular family members, about hair. This became clear in the following statement that Eve made as we discussed the issue of self-hatred in hair alteration. Eve made the following comments about the tension that hair raised between her and her mom.

EVE: I just remember like straightening my hair, and you know when it starts to grow out, my mom telling me that my kitchen [hair at the nape of neck] was kinky, "You need to touch up your kitchen." And I would just get so pissed off. This is the hair God gave me! And just being pissed off at my mom for saying that because she has like soft, curly, like the "good hair." She has the good hair. And I'm like, well, you know, hey, this is it.

Eve also addressed this tension when the women talked specifically about "good hair" and "bad hair." Her irritation with her mom arose again.

EVE: Good hair, bad hair, that's my whole life because my mom has the "good hair," and my brother had good hair too. And then there was me and my other brother and sister and it was like the curse on my poor mom to have these kids with this "bad hair" that she had to deal with. And so you hear it your whole life. And so I tell her, "You just need to stop saying that, that's just ridiculous to be callin' people's hair good and bad," you know, trying to correct her.

Eve illustrated the oppressive nature of describing hair as "good" or "bad." Parents like Cathy Wright, who made the statement that the story in *Nappy Hair* made neither her nor her daughter feel good, can play a big part in perpetuating certain notions about hair.

I would be reluctant to argue that a four-year-old has the faculty to understand the insidious and problematic aspects of "good hair" and "bad hair," but one of the first things that kids learn is the difference between anything that's good and bad. Even if they defy rules and do something bad, kids understand the consequences—they understand the rewards and punishments attached to behavior. When black children receive the message that they have "bad hair," for example, they process it through the perspective of fewer years than adults. At least theoretically, adults are able to challenge these distinctions on a personal and broader level, as Eve showed when she asked her mom to stop using "good hair" and "bad hair" terminology. But most black children are not yet able to make such an intervention. Such distinctions may inflict great damage on the self-esteem of kids who don't have "good hair." Furthermore, kids with "good hair" will continue to engage in the oppressive distinction that leads to the perpetuation of these beliefs.

Adrianna also discussed the tension that hair elicited in her family, particularly because her mother is white and was unwilling to learn the grooming practices for black hair. Adrianna explained the circumstances under which she first became aware of hair.

ADRIANNA: I guess I was four when I got it cut off and then I was just amazingly aware. And the T-shirt thing, I used to just look in the mirror with the T-shirt and just be like, if this could just be it, you know, and then I'd pull it off. I don't remember when it was longer and it was being tugged at or whatever. But then once it was cut off, it was a fight, it was a family struggle, too, between my aunt and my mom. So my hair became this symbol of the tension of like my mom not

willing to learn about black hair. [She took the stance] I don't
need to know. This is my child. Instead of saying, "Well, I
need to know what to do with it," and listen to this other family member, but she didn't.

Adrianna not only explains how she was influenced at an early
age by long hair, but how her hair became a site of cultural and
familial tension, particularly between her white mother and black
aunt. This tension demonstrates how intercultural ideas and practices about hair often clash because hair functions differently in
different groups. Furthermore, Adrianna was not only a black
child, but a black *girl,* and therefore the tension involved both
race and gender. It is not Adrianna's father or another black male
figure in the family with whom Adrianna's mother battles: it is a
black woman whose ideas about hair have shaped a broader understanding of cultural practices among her peers.

Her point is also tied to parenting and to the rights of parents
to exercise control over their children. Implicit in Adrianna's account is that her mother resented any kind of outside interference
with regard to her ability to rear her child, or, more specifically,
to groom her. Still, Adrianna's mother's reluctance can be associated with something unfamiliar, which can be further read as the
insecurity of a white mother in providing for her black daughter,
as well as racial differences and what they say about broader social forces. Research has shown that, in general, blacks and whites
see the world differently (Feagin and Sikes 1994). In the 1990s,
Americans have witnessed these differences firsthand through
the legal system. The trial that acquitted the four police officers
of beating Rodney King, and O. J. Simpson's acquittal in his crim-
inal case, left a clear picture of the racial divide between U.S.
blacks and whites. Indeed, the realities and understandings about
race mean different things for blacks and whites, underscoring
the battle between Adrianna's mother and aunt.

As noted in Adrianna's comments at the beginning of this chapter, her first haircut was a pivotal moment in her life. She continued to reflect on this moment and subsequent ones in her life.

ADRIANNA: I had it really long up 'til I was like four and then
my mom like, she couldn't deal or comb it right, so I cried. So

she took me into this white shop and they cut it all off. So I had an instant 'fro, you know, like at almost five. So I always had this thing about short hair because I was called "boy" and "Afro" and all this stuff. So I prayed every night. I just wanted long hair. I can still remember saying, like, "Oh God, please make my hair pretty tomorrow." So like by fourth grade I had a relaxer. And I was learning how to like do all the kinds of stuff with the hair dryer and the curling iron at like ten, which is ridiculous. Kids should just be in braids, or shorter, just enjoying life.

Adrianna's discussion dramatically demonstrates the relationship between hair and ideas about gender and race. She was not only called a boy because of her short hair, but she understands that for women short hair is not pretty or feminine. The nickname "Afro" is associated with hair in terms of racial identity; more specifically hairstyles show that race and gender intersect (Davis 1994; Craig 1997; Kelley 1997). Adrianna explained that hair becomes central in the lives of black girls at a very early age. It is unsettling to know that a girl so young can be stigmatized by comments that call her a boy and reduce her to a hairstyle (Davis 1994). It also points out that long hair is often associated with femininity and short hair with masculinity. Adrianna also mentioned during the interview that these comments came from kids her own age, illustrating that constructions of gender are important in the early socialization of individuals.

Adrianna feels that girls should be allowed to be girls (i.e., kids) and enjoy life instead of praying for long hair and attending to grooming practices that involve hair dryers and curling irons at such a young age. Her personal experience illustrates that psychological and practical issues impeded her ability to "just be a kid,"because even before black girls reach puberty they understand the importance of hair. Appearances are important in our society and shape how individuals view themselves, so it is not surprising that Adrianna and other women understand at an early age that beauty is important. When constructions of beauty and gender are attached to race, they shift and become associated with ideas about what it means, in this case, to be a black girl or woman within mainstream U.S. beauty culture.

Like the other focus groups, these women discussed issues that specifically focused on black girls. They were particularly critical of the message that girls receive at a young age that straight and long hair is the only kind of attractive hair. While discussing the relationship between femininity and hair, Allison made the following remarks.

ALLISON: I mean, little girls now walking around with hair weaves. I can't believe that. Little girls with the extension braids and the big bows in school. I am amazed. But to see a little girl who doesn't even know any better, or even know the difference.

GROUP: She knows.

ALLISON: Well, *she knows*. But this little girl had to be six years old just the other day and had braids down to [her back]. That's scary. This child doesn't know any better. And what if a child may have liked their short hair? You know what I'm saying? I'm sure there are cases in which children may like their short hair. But I saw this little girl and I thought, my God, she's only six. What is she going to think by the time she's ten? That there is no other way?

Allison's comments and the response of "she knows" by the group showed a recognition that girls at such a young age have both a conscious and an unconscious awareness of what it means to have long and straight hair. Indeed, black women understand the meanings of race and gender without any formal teaching (Hill Collins 1990). The consensus of Allison and the other women that young girls "know" about the social meanings of hair was really the affirmation of an implicit understanding, a given, that the socialization process that governs hair begins at a very early age. In her remark after the group said "she knows," Allison, although she acknowledged that "she knows," challenged the notion that a girl so young could *"know any better."*

Allison suggested that knowing or being cognizant of something on a conscious level does not mean that a conscious recognition of what long, fake hair *really* means can be transferred to a six-year-old—that she does not know the broader implications of why she has that long, pretty hair. She does not *know any better* because she is already a victim of a beauty culture that fosters long hair as representing femininity, and therefore beauty. When the girl turns ten, one can speculate along with Allison that she will see other images, but these will not be ones that are praised within the beauty culture, especially in a society that privileges straight, long (blonde) hair.

Allison's comments render adornment practices or, as Mercer (1990) argues, black hairstyling practices as "cultural artifacts," invisible. Parents or guardians may well argue that hair is just another way of adorning their daughters. However, weaves and braid extensions on young girls suggest that, to be beautiful, hair has to be added. Here, adornment is linked to adding something, not to maintaining what one already has. The days of adorning black girls' hair with only barrettes, bows, beads, and rubberbands may be ending as the twenty-first century approaches. In many cases,[8] girls barely out of diapers are wearing braid extensions, which speaks to the huge social investment placed on hair—an investment in hair one has to buy and an investment in long hair.

The Physicians' Group

The Physicians Group consisted of three doctors who are friends. All of the women reside in Los Angeles. Ginger, who is forty-three, was born in Detroit and raised in Los Angeles. She wears her hair very short and relaxed. Gretchen is forty-seven and was raised in Portsmouth, Virginia. She relaxes her hair and wears it in a medium to long style. Wixie is forty-five and was born in New Haven, Connecticut, and was raised both there and in Los Angeles. She wears her hair relaxed in a medium-length style.

The session took place at Ginger's house, the same site of the Teen Group session.[9] Ginger arrived a short while after I had finished my individual interview with Elisa, her daughter. Ginger was my contact person and graciously volunteered her house as the meeting place. As I began filling out Ginger's demographic information sheet, Gretchen and Wixie arrived. They read the consent forms and filled out a demographic information sheet while

we ate some snacks and I gave them some more background about 123
my project. We then retired to the same place where the teen session would commence a little later that afternoon.

Hair Does Matter

Unlike the Early Twenty-Something Group that debated the significance of hair, these women did not question the fact that hair
matters. All agreed that it does, as Wixie's comment at the beginning of this chapter illustrates. In addressing the question, two
topics emerged: swimming and the relationship between the Afro
and the Black Power movement. All of the women discussed hair
and its relationship to political and historical shifts, and how
these shifts influenced black hairstyling practices among young
blacks growing up during the 1950s and early 1960s, coming of
age during the Black Power movement.

GINGER: I know as I was growing up there was so much work
    involved in pressing that hair on Saturday night. You knew
    you could not go swimming during the week because it
    would be jacked [messed up] and your mother would be too
    through by that point. So once you realized there were certain
    things you couldn't do because of your hair then you realized
    that it must be such a big deal because you'd watch Esther
    Williams and these people do the little water ballet thang, and
    nobody was worried about pressing their hair. And that's as a
    kid growing up in the '50s and '60s. So it was a big thing and
    then for it to finally change when we got to high school with
    black power and everyone doing the natural thang. And then
    there was a whole 'nother thang with those who had the
    straight hair. Were they down with the Movement because
    they didn't have a 'fro?

Ginger provides a personal and historical map that traces black
hairstyling practices from the point of view of someone from her
generation. She mentions the pressing of hair, which always
seemed to be a weekend ritual that many of the women recalled.
Ginger presents an image of Esther Williams, who could jump

into the pool, do her synchronized-swimming routine, and emerge from the water without the pressing comb looming in the background. She illustrates how black women have come to know what they can do and can't do in relationship to how will their actions, especially those dealing with sports, affect their hair. There is also an understanding of what they perceive they *can't* do and what white women *can,* in this case, swimming. This difference provided a point of reference for Ginger in her realization that hair was, as she noted, a big deal, unlike for the Esther Williams "types."

Ginger also engages the idea of change and how the trend away from pressing hair was facilitated by the Black Power movement. She explains that the change was a big deal because it moved away from what she and other girls and women in her generation had known before the late 1960s. The Black Power movement influenced ideas about identity, beauty, and politics (Golden 1983; Wade-Gayles 1993; Davis 1994; Craig 1997). Furthermore, hair and hairstyles were an indicator of one's politics, one's commitment to the movement, and this relationship between hair and notions of blackness was something that everyone in Ginger's generation understood. According to Ginger's last comment above, hair was *the* signifier of one's politics. People wore their politics on their head, and hair spoke through you and for you. If your hair was straight, could you still be down with black political struggle?

Wixie followed up on Ginger's comments by also discussing the historical shifts that black hairstyling practices have gone through and the ideologies that went along with those shifts. Yet like Carolivia Herron's position in the aftermath of the P.S. 75 incident, Wixie explained her disappointment that black people had not rejected particular ideas about hair despite the intervention of the Afro and black (natural) as beautiful.

WIXIE: It all makes statements and at different historical times it would make a statement about you (i.e., the times of the 'fro); the standard of beauty and everybody at one point wanting long, straight hair; the good hair, the bad hair syndrome. There's really no escape, I think. I had hoped at the time of the Afro we had made the escape, but we actually did

not. There was a small blip, but after the blip we just [fell off].
It didn't go back, thank God, to the way it was, and now there
are several hairstyles with twists to 'fros, to straight or whatever.

In raising the issue of escape in relationship to hair issues, Wixie
points to ideas about freedom. She explicitly relates freedom to
the Afro and that she had hoped it would help black women escape standards of beauty that celebrate long, straight hair as well
as ideas about "good hair" and "bad hair." The Afro was only a
"blip" of an intervention, a small moment in time that could not
stand still and stave off the acceptance of "straight as right"
among U.S. blacks.

Although the Afro was a small blip, Wixie understands that it
was still significant. As she noted, hairstyling practices did not
move into a state of reversal. In fact they went forward, shaping
today's hairstyling practices. Wixie's comment in relationship to
the Afro as a blip also relates to the discussion in the next chapter on the movement of black hairstyling practices in the 1990s.
For example, Wixie explained her joy in the fact that hairstyling
practices did not go in reverse once the Afro died out. The movement forward is demonstrated today with twists, braids, dreadlocks, the Afro, to name a few, as well as straightened styles.
Wixie reflected on the idea that the Afro gave black women some
choice. Clearly, it did not overtake straight styles, but it allowed
women of Wixie's and subsequent generations the freedom to
choose from a variety of hairstyles. The choice that the Afro offered has become a much more indelible marker on hairstyling
practices than on politics among black women.

Wixie's comment below is also somewhat of a followup to Ginger's discussion about swimming and hair. However, Wixie offers
a different view of the perception that black women envy the "Esther Williams types."

WIXIE: It's always been a matter of time for me. But people
would say, well, you have straight hair or you don't have
straight hair [and what it all means]. To be quite frank, I
never envied white women's hair. I envied the time suppos-
edly they didn't have to spend with their hair 'cause I love to

swim. I want to be able to jump into the pool whenever I want. And it seemed like they had the luxury of doing that and then just flipping that hair back or whatever and going, while black folk [didn't].

Instead of framing the "envy" that black women may have for the texture of white women's hair, Wixie argues that envy is associated with time. By challenging the myth that black women want white women's hair texture, Wixie provides an alternative explanation that involves time. Her explanation about envy illustrates that something desirable is often complicated by something less obvious that can be just practical. Wixie's comment also affirms a finding of my research: black women see the issue of manageability as the key factor of "good hair" and straight hair. Black women see manageability and therefore *spending less time* as significant factors in wearing particular styles or having certain hair textures. They want hair to be less of a burden or no burden at all.

With regard to swimming, Gretchen's comments were similar to Ginger's and Wixie's, particularly in relationship to swimming and the Afro, but she provided a personal anecdote about "pretty" hair. She began with a discussion about how black girls learn at a young age what is considered pretty, but by the time they grow up, shifts occur in the perception of what is considered beautiful.

GRETCHEN: I'm sure I don't swim now because as a child it was just too much trouble to learn how to swim and the whole notion of your hair getting wet. But I do remember as a child too, you know, straight hair went along with being light skinned and that made you pretty. And even girls who were not necessarily light skinned, but if you had straight long hair, you were still considered one of the pretty girls. Two of my dearest friends were sisters. One had that braid down to your butt straight hair and the other one had very curly pretty hair. I remember women saying, "Oh, they all have," you know, somehow trying to include me when it really wasn't appropriate, "They've all got pretty good hair." And then when the Afro came along, you know, those of us who were so fortunate because we could get the biggest, baddest

Afros. And those with straight hair were going through a lot of trouble. I mean alcohol in the hair and everything else to get that nappy look.

Similar to her friends in the Physicians Group, Gretchen provides an analysis of how perceptions about black hairstyling practices have changed over time. She begins by noting that when she was a kid during the 1950s, long straight hair was considered "pretty." Therefore she was excluded from the group of girls whose hair was deemed "pretty" or "good." Like Raine,[10] of the same generation, Gretchen explains how long, straight hair often had the ability to trump skin color when classifications of "good hair" and pretty girls were made.

Once the Black Power movement ushered in "Black is Beautiful," Gretchen and countless other black women were "vindicated" for not having "pretty" or "good" hair. The long straight and curly hair that had been idolized by blacks in the 1950s and earlier was rejected by a generation of blacks influenced by the Movement. By noting that those with the stuff that Afros are made of were seen as "fortunate," Gretchen demonstrated that blacks with tightly coiled hair had no trouble sporting the "biggest" and "baddest" Afros. In contrast, those with "good hair" tried to step into the 1960s and 1970s by sporting the Afro through any means necessary, such as using alcohol in their hair. This was the beginning of a new era and acceptance of a new, nappy head of hair. Ideas about hair are not static—what hair means today may not be what it will mean tomorrow.

Occupation Matters

Another topic that surfaced during the discussion among the physicians involved issues about hair in relationship to rewards and punishments. I asked the women if they thought a relationship existed between rewards and punishments, and their response as a group can be attributed to their being doctors and the sense of autonomy they feel they have at work. Ginger began by saying that their friends who are attorneys are much more confined to rules and regulations that govern how they must present themselves at work. The following is a transcript of part of their discussion.

GINGER: We're all physicians and there's a different kind of mentality when you're a physician. You want the independence. When you work in a corporate type of environment, or a law firm, that whole culture says you wear skirts a certain length, you don't wear open-toe shoes. They really expect a certain look. When you're a physician even working in an environment that we work in as an HMO-type of thing, we still think we have more freedom because if your work is good, [that's all that matters]. As a physician, even if you're not in private practice, you can do whatever you want to do. We've done wigs, we've done weaves, we've done everything. I've been blonde, and they say, "Hmm?," you know, [but that's it]. So I don't think it's [an issue of] reward/punishment because the people who we are relating to need to come see us. They don't care about how you look. "Can you help me with my breathing or my heart?" [That's what they want to know]. They don't trip.

GRETCHEN: When you think about our friends who are lawyers, [you're right]. I've seen so many more of our friends who are physicians who have had braids and everything else. But I don't see our friends in law.

WIXIE: Yes, we have our hair every way.

GINGER: We can do that. The lawyers can't. The corporate types can't do that. Because their rewards are distinctly tied to what those other higher-ups, who are white men, think of them and how they feel about them. Whereas we don't have such higher-ups. I mean, you have the chief of your department but it's not that serious. He doesn't make that much more than you, you know what I'm saying? And that's why I went into medicine. I didn't want anyone telling me what to do or how to look or any of those other kinds of things. I wanted to be kind of in charge and I always felt that being a radiologist, everyone had to come to me. So I didn't have to kowtow to the surgeons and all that kind of crap like you would as an anesthesiologist. When I was a flight attendant, granted this was a thousand years ago, but to hear those sisters ultimately would have to go to court and go through those issues because they wanted to wear braids. And you know, when you're flying and you're changing planes and all that kind of stuff, you can't be trippin' about [hair]. If you're in Istanbul, ain't nobody pressin' no hair.

This discussion demonstrates how ideas about the relationship between autonomy and hair have more to do with occupation (doctors versus attorneys in this case) than with socioeconomic status. These physicians have more freedom to do as they please with their hair, from wearing wigs to going blonde, but their friends who are attorneys have more restrictions placed upon them because of their work environment. When Ginger made the remark about skirt length, she anticipated a fall 1998 episode of the one-hour weekly comedy/drama *Ally McBeal* on the Fox Network. McBeal, a Harvard Law graduate, is found in contempt of court by a male judge for wearing short skirts to court. In protest, Ally continues to wear short skirts to court and is thrown in jail on at least two occasions. The broader point that Ginger reflected on is that no matter how much money women may make, it is the work environment and occupation that determines your hairstyles and dress.

As a former flight attendant, Ginger's job left her little time to deal with hair. The fact that black female flight attendants had to fight legal battles to wear braids[11] in the late 1980s seemed ridiculous to Ginger because of the practical efficiency of braids, as well as the often limited access to salons that cater to black women in, say, a place like Istanbul. It appears that occupations involving contact with the public confer greater restrictions on black hairstyling practices. One of the arguments that employers used in 1980s court cases was that braids were perceived as unattractive and possibly even threatening, thereby making passengers feel uncomfortable.[12]

Still, the issue is complicated further because most doctors have just as much contact with people as flight attendants and as most attorneys. What then are the underlying factors that account for issues that relate to rewards and punishments? Clearly, it is not one factor, but a complex of many, though work autonomy seems to be a major one. Regardless of class status or occupation,[13] an environment in which autonomy is encouraged or secured allows more choice in hairstyling practices among black women.

"I Have to Be Back in the O.R. in One Hour"

I asked the women if there were any other issues that they were interested in addressing before our session ended. The following discussion focused on beauty salons and how they have become a hindrance to professional black women. Gretchen and Ginger felt that, unlike hairstyling practices themselves, beauty salons within black communities have remained stuck in a time warp. The following is an analysis of beauty salons in relationship to middle-class black women, and the economic ramifications of a relationship that has been severed.

GRETCHEN: What about beauty salons, the black beauty salons?

GINGER: In our day, that was really a culture. And you got to go to a real black beauty shop. Forget the salon, it's a black beauty shop.

GRETCHEN: And also we stayed all day. I think it's a big transition for people now. Professional women like ourselves, but just women in general, the notion of going to stay in a beauty salon or shop for three and four hours is just, is something that can absolutely not happen anymore. And I think for me, for a lot of black shops that I've been in where people still go and sit all day. They'll go and the hairdresser will straighten a few people or press a few people, and then she'll curl several others. So you really actually go and *stay*. And you have lunch and people sit and they chat and for me, that's just not a lifestyle that I can deal with.

GINGER: It's a time issue. We just don't have that kind of time. But when we were growing up there was something else happening because you had all these women telling stories about their boyfriends and hearing all this knowledge that you could never get because when you were with your parents at church, that was a little subgroup. But when you went to the

beauty shop then you had like a range of sisters 'cause like
back in the day before we could go to salons, you knew your
professional women went to the salons. The regular women,
everybody went to the salon. I mean, the same old beauty
shop. I remember sitting up there listening to those things
'cause as a little kid you didn't have any pull so really you
were down on the list as to who had to get in and out [of the
shop].

GRETCHEN: But I think that has resulted in some professional
Black women leaving some black shops that still operate the
same way.

GINGER: Oh, you can't do it now [sit in the salon all day].

GRETCHEN: But I'm saying that when you see some of the
black shops may be losing clientele and some people might
make a comment about "Well, that black woman, she only
gets her hair done in Beverly Hills now, she only goes to Hol-
lywood to get her hair done." It's not that she somehow has
taken herself out of the [community] or thinks she's above
these people. It's really to get her hair done in an hour as opposed to three or four hours, that's it. You're assured that people in the community know how to do black hair. But what I
think drives a lot of people away from these shops is because
the culture in the shops has not changed, whereas the times
have.

The conclusion emerged that these women could not sit for
hours in a beauty salon, but that the culture of beauty salons has
not changed, causing a disconnection between them and middle-
class black women. Gretchen also described fondly how, when
she was a kid, the black beauty shop, unlike church, was a place
in which class divisions were less visible and where women
talked about interesting things. It was alive with knowledge and
stories that intrigued black girls, making being the last on the list
to get your hair done bearable. Hair therefore rooted, so to speak,
the different women together with their wisdom and anecdotes.
Ginger framed her response within nostalgic notions of beauty
shop culture and how it socialized hair as well as girls themselves.

Gretchen was just as passionate in her response. Although she
noted how she and other professional black women just don't

have the time to sit and wait while one person works on several heads, there is still a sense that she regrets the fact that she has to go outside of the black community to get her hair done. The fact that she and other black women who share her position are often seen as "uppity" is troubling to Gretchen. She would prefer to go to shops in the community because, as she explained, not everyone can do black hair, and by going to a black shop, black women are more confident that they will be satisfied with the results. But professional black women like Gretchen take their chances by going to places like Beverly Hills rather than sit for hours in an old-fashioned black beauty shop. Gretchen, Ginger, and Wixie are examples of the gains that many black women have made in this society. Still, much of the rich tradition of beauty shops is a cultural phenomenon that black people want to preserve as a black cultural "institution," a place within black communities that has served to socialize black girls.

Black beauty shops are everywhere in black communities. The money to be made by investing in black hair care is phenomenal. Blacks spend millions of dollars on hair care annually.[14] In fact, salons have become specialized in the 1990s. There are salons that cater only to natural hair; others cater to braids, and still others to relaxed styles. Some may cater to all black hairstyling practices. The physicians' argument that they have more freedom about how to groom themselves for the workplace compared to their peers who are attorneys suggests that occupation is more important than class status in understanding why hair matters among black women, though their middle-class status cannot be overlooked. The fact that professional black women have the choice and means to go outside of the community to get their hair done is indicative of their middle-class privilege.

The result is that black shops have lost customers. These shops no doubt do not see the lost in terms of bodies and money because there are many black women, including middle-class ones, who continue to frequent them. So what would be the incentive for these shops to change with the times? Because many black women are still willing to make the investment of time and money, whether their time schedule permits or not, there is no incentive for black shops to change with the times. Furthermore, much like Ginger's comments about physicians providing a service that people need, the same can be said for the "doctors" of black hair. The millions of dollars that are spent on hair care actually nurture and encourage the continuation of what these women perceive as dated black (hair care) cultural practices.

Low-Income Group

Like the other focus groups, the Low-Income Group was very spirited and reflective about hair and black women. Though all of the women in this group were friends, unlike the other groups these women were from diverse generations. All are neighbors in the southwest part of Washington, D.C. All are unemployed, and except for Mary, receive some form of public assistance. Joanne is a fifty-one-year-old unemployed licensed practical nurse. She wears a short hairdo and blowdries it to obtain a straight look. Esther is thirty-seven and wears her hair in a short permed style. Mary is an unemployed forty-seven year old with medium-long cornrows. Maxine wears her hair short and permed and is thirty-three. Shaneesha is sixteen and is currently enrolled in an adult education program to earn her GED. She wears long, silky dreads and is Maxine's daughter. All of the women agreed that hair matters. Mary voiced the general sentiment of the group.

MARY: I think it's a big deal because to me, hair brings out the
    potential in a woman. If your hair is nappy, it's something
    about your expression, it don't look right. If your hair is
    probably, you now [looking nice], then it does something to
    the individual. You know I'm not sayin' it's for a beautifica-
    tion thing, but it just makes them more like, you know [it
    raises their self-esteem].

Later during the session the entire group agreed that if a black woman's hair does not look nice or well groomed, then she does not look nice or well groomed. Mary used nappy hair as an example of hair that doesn't look right or nice. By relating hair grooming to self-esteem but not to beauty, Mary attempted to make a distinction between feeling good about oneself and feeling beautiful. However, Mary does not take into consideration that self-esteem and beauty are related. Nappy hair just doesn't look right, as Mary explained, but it is also not viewed as beautiful, which has implications for how black girls and women feel about themselves, as Herron's *Nappy Hair* illustrates.

Dolores followed up in her response as to why hair matters by discussing several issues. She explained how racial identity and some hair-grooming practices among blacks not only deny an allegiance to black identity, but are unhealthy as well.

DOLORES: Black women's hair is just hair. But see, I always only deal with white people's hair. White people always wanna look like black people. Now black people wanna look like white people. The thing is, can they [blacks] keep the culture together and let blacks still know who blacks are throughout all the colorin', dyin', the tippin', the frostin'. I want you to understand black people can do that, bleach their hair blonde, but they have a lot of aftereffects after its done. And basically you don't have the chemistry and the chemicals they use on your hair and the complexion, it doesn't blend in and then they end up losing their hair; when they put tracks and stuff in it they're allergic to the glue.

Dolores wonders if the hairstyling practices among black women that she relates to "looking white" will lead them to reject their culture. She is in agreement with the other women in the group that hair says something about oneself, but she also expresses a concern that related to hair alteration, which led the discussion in that direction.

Self-Hatred?

After I asked the women if hair alteration is a form of self-hatred, Dorlores began the discussion by explaining how the same methods are used on white people's hair, but she seems to suggest that no one questions *their* motives. Shanesha followed up by explaining that hair alteration, particularly straightening, is not related to black women's desire to be white. The following is taken from

DOLORES: They [white people] have curly hair and I have put
lots of perms, liquid perms, to straighten all that fuzz ball out.
And then went to a black chemical relaxer and straightened
the white people's hair with it.

SHANESHA: I think black people, we the most luckiest people
because of our hair. Like, many people can do different things
with their hair, no matter what kinda texture it has. [Refer-
ring to one of the women] like your hair, see what I'm sayin',
your hair might be thick or whatever but you can find something else different to do with your hair. It's not [at] all about
[trying to act white] because I've permed my hair or straightened it or something because, I'm sayin' it'll get real straight
and then you can style it more different types of ways. Or
when I don't perm it I probably might get it cornrowed or
plait it up something. [It's about] just [doing] different things.

INGRID: Why do you wear your hair the way that you do?

MAXINE: Because I want to [I like it this way].

DOLORES: I wear my hair like this because it's very convenient.
It's easy. You can take baths, blow-dry your hair, pull it back,
and you don't have to do nothing else to it. And then you put
it up, pull it down, and do anything you want with it. Basically, I like simple hairstyles. Except for a special occasion.

INGRID: And simple for you would be what?

DOLORES: Oh, it's simple right now. Very simple. It's about as
simple as it can get.

None of the women related hair alteration to self-hatred. They
agreed with Dolores and Shanesha, and the other girls and
women, that hairstyling practices among black women are based
on versatility, personal choice, and convenience.

First Recognition That Hair Matters

I asked the women at what age they began to notice that there
was something to hair. All of them initially agreed they were

five years old, and then continued to reflect on their childhood memories.

MARY: Five, yes, but really when I got into teenage [years], about twelve, startin' at twelve. You know you more concerned about your hair: "Oooh mama, my hair is so nappy, I want a perm. I want my hair to look like hers," that kind of stuff.

INGRID: When you were five, did you know something was up with hair?

MARY: Yeah, because it used to hurt! My mama used to comb my hair. I had the nappiest, shortest hair in the world and she used to just pull my hair and I used to hate my hair.

SHANESHA: My mother always used to do my hair, put it in a ponytail, braid it up. But when I got nine or ten, I started doing my hair by myself.

INGRID: And so you became more kinda aware of it?

DOLORES (intercedes): I was in the sixth grade [when I took notice of hair] because I seen my sisters. They had the press and curls and the finger waves. Well, when I went to school [one day] for this Mardi Gras [event] and I saw all of these little girls with the Shirley Temple curls, I didn't want these two pigtails and this little old flatback [style].

ESTHER: When you get seven years old [you know about hair]. Like my baby, that's a big thing. She's [almost] eight.

INGRID: And she's talking about hair? What's she saying?

ESTHER: "Oh, I don't want these ponytails. I want my hair this way, I want my hair that way." I mean, come on! She knows styles and I be like, "What's that?"

Much like the discussion among the women in the Graduate Student Group, the Low-Income Group discussed how hair mattered early in life. Mary understood that hair mattered because she had nappy hair. The knowledge of hairstyles and hairstyling practices among little girls surfaced when Esther shared her dismay when her daughter requested hairstyles that Esther had never heard of. These women recognized that little girls are influenced by what they see other little (and older) girls doing with their hair, which led us into a discussion about hair, choice, and power.

The women agreed that black women have a choice in the way they wear their hair, but Esther and Dolores disagreed about external influences, particularly parental influence. Similar to Tatiana's point during the teen discussion, Esther argued that a mother's influence was important in shaping whether or not girls can exercise choice.

ESTHER: Your mother [has a say] as long as you're under her roof.
DOLORES: Boyfriends try [to have a say], but [they] are like your parents so you don't really have to pay them any attention but you try to compromise a little. Maybe he might like it short, so you wear it short a little. But if you want to go all the way, you just cut it all off [if that's what you want to do].

Though Dolores recognizes the importance of compromise, unlike Esther, she argues that parents and boyfriends are inconsequential when it comes down to hairstyling choices. In the end, it's up to black women to make those choices, and indeed they do. As we discussed choice a bit more, I asked the women if power was associated with hair. They focused on professional women in particular and raised the same issue of time and efficiency that emerged among the physicians.

ESTHER: Like if you have a high-paying job, you know. You don't never see a woman getting paid a whole lot of money with short hair.
MARY: Are you sure?
ESTHER: Not too many.
MARY: Yes, you do. A lot of high-paid administrators, presidents, you know, are wearing their hair short.
ESTHER: They're wearing a lot of weaves.
MARY: No! You better look in those black magazines and see the short, slick haired 'dos that they're wearing and it's making them look distinguished. Very distinguished.
DOLORES: I feel that these ladies have gotten older and they then start havin' children because they waited until their late

thirties to start their families and they don't want that long hair anymore. They need something so they can get in the shower—quick, quick, quick—and get to work.

INGRID: Like a practical thing?

DOLORES: That's right. That's why the hairstyle today for the businesswoman is very practical. Anywhere you go, the woman is gonna have a practical hairstyle. They not gonna get up in the morning and have to spend two hours on their hair. Twenty minutes at the most.

The women in the Low-Income Group related hair and power to occupational and economic success. While Esther argued that women with short hair are not in high-paying occupations, Mary challenged this position, saying there are real images in black magazines of successful, distinguished black women wearing short hairstyles. When Dolores chimed in, she hit the heart of a matter that middle-aged black women with career security have discussed (Nelson 1997). Though Dolores explained her point in terms of practicality, her observation that in general professional black women have opted to secure a career first and family later in fact reflects the current trend. Time and efficiency are thus only part of the picture, which we will try to make more complete in the Conclusion.

chapter 5

Black Hair, 1990s Style

I don't think that there's
necessarily a particular social
movement like the Black Power
movement that's going on. I
think there is a social climate
that encourages, that is, is
receptive to be who you are,
as you are.

Kaliph

I think all of these things that
we're [doing now with our hair]
is not a contemporary [thing].
It's nothing new under the sun.
But I do think that there's a
different sense of awareness that
we as black women have now
that has been built on the
foundations established by
our elders.

Ndeye-ante Diop

Hairstyles change like the
clothes and everything else.
Mrs. Franklin

I think we're starting to express
our individuality. So now I think
we're coming into an age of
flexibility for ourselves where
we're not letting someone else
determine for us so much what
is black, what is not black. I
think we're in a moment of self-
definition. We're allowing
ourselves to express ourselves
and feeling good about being
black and all our different
blacknesses. But I really
think it's about expressing
individuality and accepting
ourselves.

Aria

In tracing black hairstyling practices during the twentieth
century it becomes clear that in the 1990s a variety of hairstyling practices have come on the scene, much of it among U.S.
black youth culture. The influence of hip-hop culture and
rap music and videos has been tremendous on the styles of
black youth, and hair, along with clothes, dance, and lingo has
been central in setting style. Rap music videos of the 1990s

highlighted diverse hairstyling practices among blacks. Many of the natural styles that have emerged[1] and reemerged[2] were first seen in popular music videos by rap and R&B artists. In addition, there has been a resurgence of cultural nationalism in the form of Afrocentrism in the last fifteen years within black popular culture[3] and in academic circles.[4] However, this emergence cannot alone account for the variety of black hairstyles at the turn of the millennium.

Straightened styles have been a constant in the twentieth century, but the Afro emerged on a grand scale only in the late 1960s to early 1970s, and braids peaked in the late 1980s and 1990s. During the 1990s, all of these styles, along with several others, existed simultaneously. Straight styles such as the bob and French roll also found favor in the 1990s. Natural styles, whether in the form of long or short Afros, or shorter natural styles, as well as dreadlocks and twists, were just as common in the late 1990s as straight styles.

Given the variety of styles in the 1990s, I asked the girls and women why they think such variety occurred at this particular moment in history. One of the most common responses was that the 1990s were a time in which individuality was in vogue, as reflected in Kalpih's comment at the beginning of the chapter. Jean commented that "in America, we really promote the whole 'I'm an individual' thing," and Elisa made the following comment.

ELISA: I think because in the 1990s you hear a lot on TV about freedom of choice and a lot of people, I guess, back in the day, peer pressure really kicked in, [so you just went with the times]. Whereas now I think it's sort of you do your own thing and do what you want to do.

Elisa, Jean, and Kaliph stress individuality, and Elisa and Kaliph see the 1990s as a time in which individualism was encouraged. Jean translates this observation into the general idea of individualism that pervades U.S. society. The movement is not in the form of a social movement such as Kaliph noted, but a movement of thought that promotes individual expression. In the Dennis Rodman era of individuality and originality, it's okay to be who you are, however you want to express it.

Still, when I asked Nia to address the question of why there has been such an explosion of black hairstyles during the 1990s, she explained how the effects of racism have forced blacks to express an individuality that is rooted within black cultural expression as demonstrated in hairstyling practices. She connected the variety to a movement among college-aged black youth.

NIA: There's a general trend of increased consciousness among the college-aged. But you also see it just in the rap groups and that resistance kind of movement. Part of it, I think, is that things have begun to reverse on us and the difference is becoming so clear and the resistance. You know, for a while, the 1960s came and then it kind of got contaminated and a lot of it got sold up. Just went along into corporate America and things kind of disappeared and got less important. And then they started pulling the rug back out from under us and so we started falling back. And I think the more we are confronted with racism in America, the more we're forced, if you will, into coming into our own. There's the opportunity now, everything is broader. I mean just for hairstyles, and like you said, you see everything. We didn't see everything. So I think it's the climate in America specifically. I think it's the backward movement in terms of everything black folk thought they had achieved. And that always forces us back to ourselves, thank goodness. So it's not always bad.

Unlike the previous statements about individuality, Nia's comments reflect the influence of a social climate that has nurtured black cultural expression in reaction to racism. Blacks have had to foster an individuality that must resist the attack on their civil rights. The passing of Proposition 209 in California banning affirmative action in public hiring practices and state university admissions and the equivalent I-200 in Washington State are two examples of such attacks. Nia focuses on a "backward movement" in the 1990s that is forcing blacks to understand that the evils of racism continue to pervade American society; it is a wake-up call for blacks. This "back to ourselves" reaction signals an understanding that a liberal view of race is sweeping the country at the end of the twentieth century. The argument that race does not matter and that the playing field is level for all Americans feeds into the conservative and color-blind rhetoric of anti–affirmative action pundits. Nia sees the consciousness among the younger generation, and the influence of rap music, as a resistance "kind of movement" that serves as a buffer against the walls that have been closing in on the gains that blacks have achieved in the past, particularly in the 1960s. By reading hair as a medium through which empowerment and resistance are nurtured, Nia explains that cultural expression is politicized in the current political climate. Whereas the connection between hairstyling practices and resistance may not be as obvious as it was during the 1960s and 1970s, Nia shows that hair merely reflects political shifts that are shaping the lives of blacks.

Sheila related the variety in black hairstyling practices to natural styles this way.

SHEILA: I think that as more of us become more aware of ourselves and our own identity and as we begin to realize and accept more of our own culture, I think we start to change about our hair. It's a mind shift that you go through and it happens when you realize you've come to a point where you really become aware that your philosophy about hair impacts so much more in your life than just the hair itself. We as black people, there's a lot in our culture and there's a lot in our race consciousness that we struggle with as far as, you know, living in this European society and having to accept ourselves as very un-European. And so, you come to a point where you just don't want to play that game anymore and you don't want to participate in it anymore, or at least as little as possible. And so I think the more we get to that and the more we realize that, the more we are happy with and can accept our hair as it is naturally.

Similar to Nia, Sheila discusses a "mind shift" that relates to hair and an embracing of black culture among blacks. The more that U.S. blacks understand that they exist on the fringes of American society, as reflected in Nia's discussion of racism, the more they accept, as Sheila argues, black "hair as it is naturally." Black hair in its natural state is seen as progressive. Sheila's explanation fo-

cuses on the heightened awareness or consciousness in black hairstyling practices and the acceptance of natural hair, as was already evident in the late 1960s and early 1970s in relationship to
the Afro among many blacks.

Unlike Nia's and Shiela's specific references to the relationship
between natural styles and a heightened racial consciousness,
Laurie explained how a 1990s consciousness of black women as
well as a consciousness regarding the past may be influencing the
variety of hairstyling practices among black women.

LAURIE: I think that diversity maybe has something to do with
the consciousness of black women now. And the diversity of
where our minds are. I think maybe it has much deeper meaning than just difference, than just history repeating itself.
Maybe it's repeating itself in hair, but maybe it's not the hair
that's the issue. What was the mind state of black women during that time, and how much is that resurfacing itself now?
And in particular with black women who have chosen not to
be politically correct with their hair and not to lend themselves to the white standards, if you will. And so I think that
there's a rebellion going on within that, within the hair.
Within the hair speaking for the mind and the psyche of
black women.

Like Sheila, Laurie placed the diversity that is apparent in black
hairstyling practices among black women outside of hair itself by
discussing these practices in relationship to the "mind state" of
black women and how "hair speaks for the mind and the psyche
of black women." After asking how much of a past consciousness
in black women's hair styling practices is resurfacing in the 1990s,
Laurie continues by making reference to natural styles. She also
questions whether or not recent hairstyling practices, particularly in the form of natural styles like the Afro, are loaded with
the same political and cultural meaning as in the late 1960s and
1970s. Natural styles may not reflect the politics of the late 1960s
as much as the fact that black women are moving beyond images
of beauty both in black communities and in mainstream society.
By noting that a rebellion is occurring through natural hairstyling practices among black women and that these practices can

be read as resistance, Laurie argued that such practices are indicative of a psychological movement away from mainstream standards of beauty for many black women. In making reference to the relationship between natural styles and political (in)correctness, Laurie made a historical connection in addition to demonstrating that hair is loaded with political, personal, social, and cultural baggage.

Other women also discussed the recent emergence of natural hairstyles among black women in addressing the diversity of hairstyles. Kaliph saw a more forgiving social climate as well as the political ramifications of black women wearing their hair short and natural.

KALIPH: One specific thing as to why there's more of a proliferation of black women wearing their hair natural . . . it has to do with a social climate that is receptive to it, that encourages different standards of beauty. And black women are buying into it. And more than anything else, for black women to wear their hair short and natural is political because it is a statement of empowerment, I think, and in some way, you're resisting and defying conventional standards of beauty. Although we do see a lot more [natural styles] on TV, there still is a predominant "white is right," length is good, bleach blonde, color, dye, or whatever you want to do. So I do think it can be seen as an act of resistance because it's still not glorified, per se. Although it may be more readily accepted.

Like Laurie, Kaliph does not think that late 1960s history is repeating itself in making natural styles popular among black women in the 1990s. Instead there is a "social climate" that welcomes these short and natural styles, though they may not be "glorified." This apparent contradiction demonstrates that styles that are welcomed on the level of fashion may still exist on the margins within broader and traditional ideas of what is deemed beautiful and acceptable. Still, the margin is a site of resistance where empowerment is nurtured (hooks 1984).

Ideas about fad, as noted in Mrs. Franklin's comments that open this chapter, also surfaced in discussions about the variety of hairstyles in the 1990s. Lee felt that past styles are repeating themselves, thus shaping the diversity in black hairstyling practices. She explained as follows.

LEE: People tend to repeat things [from] the past . . . that's where the styles come from. People just may see a picture from flippin' through a magazine or in the library [and think], "Ooh, I like that style." And it might start a whole sweep and everybody wants their hair like that. And they do it.

Although Lee's explanation points to fad, trend, and fashion and how they influence hairstyling practices, Dianne explained that the effect of such influence is related to advertising and how it shapes these practices.

DIANNE: Well, I think they change because society changes. They put it on television, we see it, and we go buy it, and we fall for it.

Dianne explained how blacks are duped when it comes to the influence of the media on fashion. Although style is associated with fashion, especially a good mode of fashion, the definition of style also relates to being smart. Given the insidious nature of advertisements, how are notions of style with respect to fashion and to the idea of being smart, used to dupe blacks? Times change, but by noting that "we fall for it," Dianne questions whether or not blacks have the ability to determine "style," questioning the advertisements that sell hairstyling practices to blacks. Furthermore, she relates trends in fashion to commodification, which is based on more than just styles repeating themselves over time.

Kaliph mentioned immigration and the effect that it has had on cultural practices in the United States. She used personal experience in her explanation.

KALIPH: I think also immigration has a part to do with it. And for whatever reason, I have noticed just way more African and Caribbean people in New York in the past ten years maybe as opposed to when I was first growing up. And with immigrants come new style, be it clothing and also hair.

By discussing specifically the immigration of people of African descent from other parts of the African diaspora and how such blending has shaped U.S. black hairstyling practices, Kaliph demonstrates how the Black Atlantic (Gilroy 1993) has influenced cultural practices among blacks. The introduction of new cultural practices as a result of immigration is a facet of the blending of different cultures.

Conclusion

While the media in general was fascinated by the fact that a white teacher was reprimanded after using a children's book about a black girl's hair, the point of contention among blacks was more insidious. I again encountered the concern among blacks about highlighting the issue of hair during the summer of 1999, when I spoke at a conference. One of the attendees at my talk shared a comment overheard from another black woman after she read the title of my talk. The woman commented that the reason hair is a problem in black communities is because black people are always talking about it. Implicit here is that by bringing attention to hair black people in general, and research on blacks and hair in particular, not only add to the problem, but *create* tension as well. In conversations about hair, black women are not merely discussing *hair*. These discussions point to forces that go beyond grooming practices and esthetics. At the core of these daily and seemingly casual dialogues exist complex narratives of identity politics.

Hair Matters presents another way of examining how black women construct knowledge. In the comments presented here, black girls and women illustrate their understandings of the political and material realities of black women's hair. Hair holds value, as illustrated in the comments about "good" and "bad" hair. Hair can be a badge of cultural pride, as well as simply an indicator of style. Hair can be used as a medium to maintain the status quo or go against it. Jeannette Mageo's (1994) argument that public symbols (beliefs) affect individuals personally holds true here as many of the girls and women used a personal narrative to discuss why hair matters within ideas about identity, beauty, and power. Though a great deal of the discussion in previous chapters focuses on grooming practices and the material nature of black women's hair, *Hair Matters* has attempted to get underneath these practices to understand the various forces that shape black women's lives. The comments here suggest that black girls and women use hair as a medium to understand complex identity politics that intersect along the lines of race, gender, class, sexuality, power, and beauty. For example, some of the interviewees explained how hair is a marker of feminine and sexual identity. Others explained how race and gender identities are formed through ideologies about hair. In addition, hair matters for black women are never merely arrested within esthetics. As *Hair Matters* illustrates, an examination of black women's relationship to U.S. beauty culture reveals complex, and often contradictory, ideas that black women hold about race, gender, sexuality, and power. In the following discussion, I present a summary of the chapters and highlight trends that emerged in the interviews, as well as particular topics that further delineate how hair shapes black women's consciousness about broader issues.

In chapter 1, though responses as to why hair matters crossed age categories, the senior women I interviewed discussed beauty and grooming practices whereas teens and women in their twenties to fifties discussed these points, and also the social and political aspects of black women's hair. This suggests that in part, age is a factor in how hair matters to black women. Of the senior women, Mrs. Franklin was concerned about her hair thinning with age, while her peer, Bobbie, focused on her lifelong use of the straightening comb. Both of these women agreed that hair is tied to looking presentable, and therefore being successful, a point that Raine and Tyler, both in their forties, associated with economic success. They pointed to hair as central in black people's occupational, and therefore economic, success. These two women explained how black people's ability to conform to mainstream standards of beauty is tied to being successful, a belief that was prevalent among blacks during the early part of the twentieth century (Tyler 1990).

Several of the women pointed to the relationship between 149
black women and U.S. beauty culture in assessing why hair matters. Kaliph and Indigo began their discussion by explaining how
mainstream images of beauty do not celebrate nappy hair and
how blacks are socialized to reject nappy hair as beautiful. In addition, the comments in the opening chapter set the stage for discussions about manageability and "good" and "bad" hair that
emerged in subsequent chapters. Though some of the interviewees reinforced the negative connotation applied to nappy hair,
others challenged it. These comments demonstrate that beliefs
about "good" and "bad" hair continue among blacks.

One point that stood out in chapter 1 was Jocelyn's comment
that in the late 1990s, black hair was privileged much as (straight
and blonde) white hair has been historically. Though, does appropriation and exoticization of black (popular) culture translate
into acceptance of black people and culture within the mainstream? Actually, popular acceptance does not translate into political acceptance, which might be manifested by a widespread
belief among white Americans that affirmative action was still
needed or that race mattered in U.S. society. A false sense of progressive racial U.S. politics arises when black cultural practices
that reinforce stereotypes of blacks (as entertainers, athletes, and
so on) and of accepted behavior and occupations for blacks are
translated into a "blacks have made it now" narrative. Through
rap music and hip-hop culture, black popular (youth) culture has
been very influential in the last ten years in embracing a variety
of hairstyling practices. The rise in natural styles in the 1990s can
be attributed to these hairstyles being represented in music
videos and advertisements. Though many of these styles privileged nappy hair, the contention surrounding the P.S. 75 incident
illustrates the various ways that nappy hair continued to be read
in the late 1990s. Though other interviewees focused on the devaluation of nappy hair, Jocelyn related the issue to mainstream
consumption of black popular culture, thereby providing a context for why black hairstyling practices are being imitated by
nonblacks. Jocelyn's and Habiba's comments that focus on mul-
tiracial readings of why hair matters illustrate how these two
women view the relationship between hair and politics that move
beyond the identity politics of black women.

Conclusion

One important note to make here about the statements in the opening chapter is that comments relating to men were sparse. Though a few comments were made, such as Jean's, the women interviewed here focused on other factors relating to why hair matters. This finding was reiterated in the women's comments in chapter 3 when asked if black women have a choice in the way they wear their hair. This suggests that most of the women interviewed here perceive their decisions about hair grooming as independent of what men want.

In chapter 2, the politics of black women's hair in relationship to racial and gender identity surfaced again. Is there a relationship between what black women do to their hair and self-esteem? The major finding here was that women who straightened their hair were more likely to disagree with the self-hatred account of hair alteration, whereas women wearing natural styles were more likely to agree with it. Even one's political affiliation did not indicate one's position on this subject among the women interviewed. Nia is a self-identified Afrocentrist and agreed with the self-hatred theory, whereas other women who identified themselves as proud of their racial heritage rejected the self-hatred theory. Still others, like Cheryl, illustrated how beliefs about racial pride and solidarity relate to one's understanding about what it means to be an "authentic" black woman. To a certain extent, Cheryl believes that a black woman's politics or authenticity is read through her hair, making Cheryl concerned about how she is perceived as a black woman with straightened hair but proud of her racial heritage. Other women with straightened hair, such as Andrea, were less conflicted about their politics and hair grooming practices. In fact she challenged the self-hatred theory by noting that if straightened hair makes a black woman feel beautiful, how does that translate into self-hatred? Many of the women interviewed here support Craig's (1997) argument that the self-hatred theory misses the various meanings that black women attribute to hair alteration. The reasons behind hair grooming practices among black women cannot be reduced to one thing. However, several of the comments in chapter 2 present contradictions in that some of the women supported the self-hatred theory in their attempt to subvert it. The explanations characterizing hate as too strong a word led some of the women to replace "hate" with less judgmental words or statements such as "lack of self-love." Though semantically distinct, in a broader sense these comments show that these black women buy into the relationship between hair and identity on some level.

Chapter 3 illustrated how black women understand theoretical and practical manifestations of power and choice. The various ways that the women interviewed discussed the relationship between hair, power, and choice further demonstrates how hair provides a window for understanding identity politics among black women. The comments focused on hair as empowering or disempowering for black women for reasons that span the spectrum from racial pride to the devaluation of black physical characteristics. The question focusing on whether black women have a choice in the way they wear their hair furthered the discussion about the relationship between hair and power. Most of the women stated that black women have a choice, thereby underscoring the lack of comments about men's desires in the opening statements among the women. In their discussion about the relationship among hair, power, and choice, several of the women related black women's autonomy to individual acts that go against the grain. On the other hand, disempowerment can stem from black women's relationship to mainstream beauty culture.

Craig's (1997) and Kelley's (1997) argument that gender matters in understanding the meaning of hairstyling practices among blacks was supported here as well. Some of the women suggested that black women are held to more rigid gender ideals in relationship to beauty culture than men. In addition to discussing traditional ideas about what constitutes femininity, interviewees also focused on the relationship between hair and sexuality, further illustrating how ideas about gender and sexual identity are constructed.

Though the focus-group chapter presented data from girls and women from different age categories in general, a fair number of the responses were similar across the focus groups, as illustrated in the teens' and physicians' discussion about swimming. In addition, Wixie's point that she envies the perceived time that white women don't have to spend on their hair underscored the discussion by the teens and the twenty-something groups as they debated how a central sense of freedom or flexibility is in black

Conclusion

girl's and women's understanding of why hair matters. One's hair texture appears to influence perceptions about hair and hair grooming practices as demonstrated in the discussion by the teen and twenty-something groups. As the girls and women discussed having "good" hair vis-à-vis their peers with tightly coiled black hair, their understanding of privilege emerged. Awareness that hair matters at an early age surfaced as well, as noted in each focus group. The physicians and low-income women discussed occupational and socioeconomic status in relationship to professional black women. The physicians' discussion suggests that occupation, not class status per se, influences black women's ability to exercise free will in their hairstyling practices. However, when these women explained that their schedules did not allow them to spend hours in a black beauty shop, it was clear that their class status afforded them the option to go outside of black communities, in this case to Beverly Hills, to get their hair done. Whereas one of the low-income women stated that she wished she had more money to get her hair done, the concern of the physicians that I spoke to focused on the lack of time that professional black women have during a given day. During the discussion with the low-income group, two of the women debated whether or not successful black women wore short hairstyles. This demonstrates that there still exists the perception that successful women wear more conventional hairdos. Dolores explained that for professional black women, wearing short hair is a practical move. Similar to the physicians' discussion about the lack of time to spend on hair given the demands of being doctors, Dolores explained how professional black women need hairstyles that allow them to focus on their careers, that is, less time-consuming styles. Whereas the investment in longer hair or even more conservative styles may have indeed been practical at the outset of their careers, this may not be the case as black women gain more autonomy or security in their occupations.

Although in general the girls and women discussed similar topics across age categories, particular issues can be attributed to age. The physicians' discussion of the Black Power movement describe their coming-of-age stories during a moment in history when blacks wore their politics on their head. The teens spent a great deal of time discussing boys and potential mates, demon-

strating the heterosexual adolescent preoccupation with the opposite sex.

In chapter 5, the girls and women illustrated that meanings of hair and hairstyling practices are not fixed. For example, depending on the person and context, nappy hair may be regarded as negative or positive. The comments in the final chapter suggest that during the late 1990s, black girls and women were more concerned about satisfying their own preferences and portraying a sense of individuality that may or may not be associated with rejecting mainstream standards of beauty. Women wearing Afros in 1999 may feel a connection to its historical roots, whereas others may see the Afro as a way to express individuality or style. Kaliph suggests at the end of the chapter that the blending of people of African descent in certain urban areas has influenced the variety in hairstyling practices. As a result, as other interviewees explained, black women are afforded more choices in how they wear their hair. The climate during the 1990s supported individuality, thereby influencing diverse styles. Thus, the acceptance of individuality and a myriad of choices nurtured diversity of hairstyling practices among black women. As Wixie explained, the Afro ushered in the choices that black women were afforded long after the late 1960s and early 1970s.

One of the most telling findings among the comments by the girls and women I interviewed is that the value that is placed on "good" hair or straightened hair has less to do with attractiveness and more with convenience and manageability. Here, the girls and women were concerned with having a certain type of texture or style that facilitates a lifestyle free of difficult or time-consuming hair grooming practices. Though some of the comments present contradictions, the fact that so many of the girls and women focused on manageability illustrate that black women have real concerns about the material nature of hair and what it means in the management of their everyday lives. Still, few women explicitly considered how their material understanding might be related to immaterial or external ideas, though many of their statements relate to how social and cultural forces shape their beliefs about hair.

When Ann explained why hair matters, she pulled together in one statement several issues that were discussed throughout the

Conclusion

interviews. Her comments below synthesize the various voices that have resonated throughout this book:

ANN: I would say as a cultural phenomenon hair, I hope, is becoming less of an issue. But I think historically we came through a time period when hair was an issue for black women simply because, and I know it's true for me, we were force-fed and bought into the European stereotype, the European standard of beauty and that meant that our (people in my generation) lives when we were children were really shaped by a variety of things. One of those things that shaped our lives that didn't have anything to do, for example, with boys of any race and with white girls, or presumably Asian girls, was what to do with our hair. Most women I know in my generation, for example, don't swim. You didn't learn how to swim when you were a little girl 'cause you could mess your hair up. You went to the beauty shop before you went to church, so that meant for us, especially for kids, you chewed up two or three or four, maybe three or four or five hours out of your day on the weekend in the beauty shop 'cause adults always went before you. So kids spent all their time in the beauty shop getting their hair done. And that was a normal way of life. I think we gained some things, but in other ways, there was the message that you had to fix yourself so in that sense I would say that [hair] was a big deal. I have a sense that it's, as I look around my friends with their children, that it's not a big deal nowadays. That it's not as, for instance, restrictive. Girls, little girls, ten years old [don't have to say] "Oh I can't go to camp because I can't do my hair!" It's not like that but one thing, chemicals are different so if you have an eight-year-old little girl, you may be relaxing her hair already—she's wearing an Afro or some other option. I mean little girls have braids now so that either you have dealt with hair or you have allowed her hair to remain natural in which case it's not an issue. And these choices seem to be there, and I think once we respect the range of possibilities, then hair becomes less of an issue. When I use the word "issue," my operational definition is something that you have to work your life around. And in my generation when we were children, girls' hair was something that you had to work your life around. It made a difference where you played, what you did, where you lived, what the deal was. I have a clear memory, for instance, of going away to summer camp when I was a little kid and having my mother (we're talking about the '50s) go directly to the kitchen (she knew where to go) and find one of the kitchen staff and got them to agree to do our hair on the weekends. So then we could be in summer camp with no problem. It wasn't about having counselors there, having professional staff there; in those days it wasn't an option (to have blacks in those positions). We were the only black children at camp, for that matter, because we lived in the North for one thing. Whereas I suspect maybe in Southern environments it wouldn't have been quite the same because there might have been more structures in place for kids. And I don't know, that's a speculation on my part . . . but I know where I lived and what I did, we went to a church camp and the time we were in church camp we were the only black kids there. And so my mom had to find somebody to do our hair. But it worked out fine. No problem. Whereas nowadays, I mean if I had a ten-year-old and I wanted to send her away to camp and there was a lake and there was swimming and there was all that kind of stuff, hey, I'd just cut her hair off and let her go natural and send her to camp and let her play all summer and that would be fine. But it's different now [than when I grew up].

Ann's comments illustrate that hair indeed shapes black women's consciousness about a host of issues. *Hair Matters* is certainly not complete in its assessment of why hair matters to black women in particular, and black communities in general. There are gaps here that could be filled by more specific analyses that focus more closely on, for example, whether or not differences within socioeconomic status and occupation provide greater detail as to why hair matters among black women. Do black women in particular occupations feel autonomous in how they wear their hair while others don't? Is there less investment in hair among black women after making partner or securing tenure? I argue in my assessment of previous literature and of the comments by many of the women that race and cultural contexts are factors. However a

Conclusion

cross-racial study might provide similar and dissimilar data among different racial and ethnic groups, and it might make the case to a greater extent that race and ethnicity matter in how groups view hair. The influence of gender is important and begs the need for a discussion that focuses on black boys' and mens' perceptions of the hairstyling practices of black men and women. Studies focusing on black beauty shops and barber shops as cultural sites where ideas about race, gender, relationships, and so on etc. are shaped would greatly expand the research on hair and it's relationship to broader issues. Studies focusing on black children and how they learn about beauty, gender, and race through hair would add greatly to future research within children's studies. The field is wide open for future examinations. One certain fact is that hair will continue to provide a window into complex identity politics among U.S. blacks, as the P.S. 75 incident illustrated so vividly. For black women, hair matters will continue to shape their ideas about personal and group identity.

Appendix I
Methods, Methodology, and the Shaping of "Hair Matters"

Background

During the fall of 1996 and winter of 1997, I completed forty-three individual interviews and four focus group interviews with African American women and girls. I conducted a fifth focus group during the fall of 1998. The interviewees consisted of girls and women ranging in age from thirteen to seventy-six, and they came from various walks of life. The individual interviews were conducted in Oakland, California; Berkeley, California; Los Angeles; Atlanta; and Santa Barbara, California. I left the choice of where each interview would take place in the hands of the women and girls.[1] Most of the interviews were in the home of respondents. In three cases, I interviewed women at my home in Oakland. One interview was conducted at a San Francisco Bay Area university, and a fair number of others at a historically black college/university in the Southeast. I also conducted one interview in my office at the time, at the Center for Black Studies at the University of California, Santa Barbara. Two focus groups were conducted in Oakland, two in Los Angeles, and one in Washington, D.C.

On average, the individual interviews lasted 35–45 minutes. Some lasted as long as 1.5 hours. On average, the focus group sessions lasted 1.5 hours. I allowed each interviewee to choose an alias before the interview began so that they would feel comfortable in choosing a name by which I would refer to them during the interview. Before each interview began, I gave a brief synopsis of my research and then handed out consent forms to participants. We then moved to completing a "demographic data sheet" that I designed for the specific personal information I collected. Only the interviewees' aliases appeared on this sheet. I designed a "confidential information sheet" to collect address information from the women and girls so that I could send them thank you notes, as well as keep them posted about the publication of *Hair Matters*. I also provided my permanent mailing address and phone numbers to the women and girls so they could stay in contact in case they moved or just wanted to drop me a note. A list of the girls' and women's aliases along with demographic data appear in table form in Appendix III. All of the sessions were audio-recorded and, as stated in the consent form, all participants could refuse to answer any question or could turn the tape off at any moment.

Recruiting, Snowball Sampling, and Focus-Group Methods

Initially I obtained five names from friends and associates who knew that I needed recruits for my study. I had already met two of these women prior to the interview. After the interviews, each woman gave me at least five names of other women I could contact, which facilitated my goal to employ snowball sampling. In fact, one Sunday afternoon and evening I "snowballed" down an entire block. The women I interviewed that day recruited neighbors and relatives that lived in close proximity. These were more senior women, so at each house I had a meal. It was Sunday afternoon, so there was lots of food to be had. As they would phone each other in their recruitment efforts, they would end by saying, "She's really thin, so feed her because she needs to eat." Each time I left a house, I would first make a trip to my car, parked on the street in front of the first interviewee's house, to drop off a plate of food before going to the next house. By the time I returned home nearly ten hours later, I was stuffed. It was interesting to hear the women explain how some of their particular dishes were better than "so-

and-so's" because "she puts too much salt in her greens" or "I
squeeze a little lemon in my sweet potato pie so it's better than
so-and-so's." This was clearly the stuff that makes any ethnography or ethnographically informed study rich.

I wanted as diverse a group of girls and women as possible. In
an effort to have various hair textures and hairstyles[2] represented
among them, I would often ask interviewees if they had friends
they could refer me to who wore their hair a certain way. In addition, I wanted as much of a range of ages as possible. I also made
an effort to include women from various educational back-
grounds and occupations. Despite my desire to have as diverse a
group as possible, I was interested in talking to anyone who
would take time out of their schedule to speak with me. Still, re-
cruiting girls and women was generally not a difficult task,
though it was difficult to find low-income women who would re-
turn my phone calls. My nonprobabilistic sampling technique of
snowballing did not work so well with low-income women. I so-
licited names from friends, associates, and key informants, but
making actual contact was often difficult because within the
course of my phoning them in a 24–48-hour period, some had
moved or their phone had been disconnected. Because of time and
financial restraints of my own, I retreated from the field after
gathering over 90 percent of my data to rethink ways of reaching
low-income women. It was important to me to gain insights from
them in order to obtain various voices and perspectives. Thanks
to the efforts of a couple of very good friends, I was still able to
conduct a focus group session with low-income women almost
two years after completing the other interviews.[3]

Although I wanted to talk to women from different walks of life
in the individual interviews, I deliberately chose to have focus
groups with homogeneous participants within each group. In
these cases the girls or women were good friends and similar in
age and educational status. This proved to be very fruitful because of the familiarity factor among the women. This strategy
was beneficial because the extra time needed to allow participants
to warm up to each other was unnecessary. All of the girls and
women had known each other for years, and over half of them had
grown up together. My entrée into their friendship circle was facilitated by my acquaintance with the woman who set up the time

and place for the meeting. All of the focus group sessions were conducted in the home of my contact.

Managing Data

When I began sifting through the data and constructing themes from the questions and responses, it became evident that several of the responses were similar. My task then was to choose one or two responses that were typical. Instead of choosing common responses randomly for particular themes, I chose comments that represented a variety of response types. Some responses were more detailed than others, but I never just chose the most detailed responses. The main criteria that I used was that any given common response that I chose was representative of that response (e.g., "good hair" and "bad hair").

Responses that were uncommon or "outliers" were easy to include. I also made a concerted effort to include a response by all of the girls and women. Some voices appear more than others for various reasons. Some girls and women were more vocal than others. Some women were more likely to discuss matters that ended up as outliers once I began analyzing the data. Still other women made statements that supported earlier studies, and others challenged them.

Black Expectations: Subject Positions and the Research Field

To begin, I expected that as a black woman my "insider status" would be completely advantageous in the field. I imagined asking follow-up questions or probes, and the discomfort that some of the girls and women might have in addressing questions about self-hatred. Until I actually hit the field, however, I did not comprehend how I could potentially shape my study precisely because of my race and gender. This discussion frames much of my discussion below. In addition, I discuss particular questions that were posed by two of the women I interviewed: "What are you going to tell us about our hair that we don't already know?" asked Raine during an individual interview, and Patricia wanted to know, "What is the significance of your study, what are you trying to prove?" during a focus group session. These questions caught me off guard and also speak to the expectations that I held as a black female social scientist.

Although we read how race, gender, class, sexuality, and so on shape the perceptions and expectations of researchers, social scientists are taught to maintain objectivity in the field.[4] It's a difficult and humbling experience when researchers admit that they had certain expectations upon entering the field. Race location and assumed racial location shapes our knowledge as researchers as well as the knowledge of the people we study. The following discussion focuses on how my expectations as a black woman conducting research about black women were based on my assumptions about race and gender.

The Academy as "White Space"

Based on my perceptions of the academy, I made assumptions about who would question my work and who would not. Through my undergraduate and graduate studies, I understood the scholarly contributions that Black Studies scholars in general, and black feminist scholars specifically, have made to academia. I understood that black people's lives were worthy of an examination that challenged and went beyond deviant-centered analyses. However, I understood that my work would be positioned as marginal among a general body of scholarship that exists within a European-centered male academy. I imagined the puzzled looks, laughs, and general skepticism that my work would receive. I imagined questions, whether they were verbalized or not, that focused on the validity of my study, its importance, and the scholarly contribution, if any, that it would make. I imagined that my research would be contained within the realm of fetish, a sexy topic that would never be received as "real" scholarship. Although black female scholars have provided wonderful discussions about how black women generate theory through their everyday discussions and actions (Christian 1988; Hill Collins 1990), I wasn't sure that a white-washed academia would get the point of my research. Black girls' and women's voices are not only marginalized or silenced within the broader U.S. society, but black female scholar's voices are marginal at best, and silenced at worst within academia (duCille 1996; Guy-Sheftall 1995; Wing 1997). Thus, my expectation of who would raise questions about my work was based on my perception of the academy as a space that was less than inviting to the voices of black women, whether textural or verbal.

The Expectation of Transparency and the Reality of Transparency

Ironically, the questioning of my work came from two black women whom I interviewed and who are not academics. Raine's question seemed to ask, "As black women, we are the experts about our hair, so what is your study going to add to what we already know?" I had been concerned about the inability of white (male) academics to see the value of my work, but here Raine, a black female, seemed to suggest that the project was *so transparent*, what's the point? Could I really add something that black women didn't already know? My reaction and reading of these questions illustrate the expectations that I held as a black woman conducting the research that is the subject of this book. As I interviewed black girls and women methodological issues emerged that relate to my being an insider. That is, as a black woman doing research about black girls and women, my race and gender linked me to the group I studied.

The questioning of my work thus came from the very "community of scholars" from whom I had least expected it. I was prepared to defend the validity of my research to social scientists and other cultural theorists, but I never expected any of the black girls or women I interviewed to challenge it. I had spent a good amount of time anticipating this question, but it was the ultimate irony when it was posed by Patricia, a black woman. Although

Raine also posed a question, it was qualitatively different from Patricia's. In fact, Raine's question did not surprise me the way Patricia's did. Although I didn't think about Patricia's question before I entered the field, I would not have been surprised if more
women had asked me the same question. But Patricia employed
the language of positivism. In asking what was I trying to prove
in my study, she explained that, as a scientist, she had assumed I
wanted to test a hypothesis. In this regard, her question did not
seem unusual, but I did not anticipate such a question with respect to the significance of hair to black women.[5]

Still Patricia's question surprised me, not because I didn't think
any of the women I interviewed were capable of putting forth a
methodological question, but because I felt that if criticism were
going to come from anywhere, it would come from the academy.
The women I interviewed, as well as some I didn't interview, had
asked many questions about my study, but no one had ever asked
what I was trying to "test" or "prove." In fact, many of the women
were quite happy that someone was finally asking them why hair
matters to U.S. black women and that my research would produce
a book. Like me, many of the women felt that it was long overdue.

Raine's query was pretty clear: black women's hair problems
are overstated. Black women have considered and talked about it
so much in their everyday lives, was there really anything new
that I could say that would actually be useful to them? On the
other hand, Patricia's query reaffirmed my view that black
women view hair differently depending on who they are. Nevertheless, I assumed that every black woman understood that hair
matters, and I was interested in discovering why it matters and to
whom. Patricia's question and subsequent discussion that night
were more fodder for my argument that hair does indeed shape
black women's ideas about race, gender, and power.

Acknowledging Advantage and
Disadvantage in the Field

One of my biggest concerns involved how I would be perceived
among the women I interviewed. I wasn't naive enough to believe

that somehow I was separate or would be treated as an "outsider"; as a black woman, I was clearly in the mix of the study despite my role as researcher. Unable to escape the various ways that black hairstyling practices are read, and considering my race and gender, I understood that I would not be a neutral researcher as a black woman.

For example, though I wear hats all the time, especially during the fall and winter seasons, I intentionally went into each interview with my hair uncovered. I felt that if I covered my head, I would be sending a message to the women that I was trying to hide something. Here they were about to discuss some very personal thoughts, yet I was unwilling to reveal what was under my cap. Granted, I understand that placing an identity on individuals based on superficial markers such as hairstyles is problematic (such as the Afro or dreadlocks among blacks as an indicator of one's politics, or a buzz cut among women as an indicator of sexual preference), but my recognition doesn't stop that practice. I understand the power of hair among U.S. blacks, and I didn't want my motives on any level questioned by the girls and women I interviewed. Though white women, for example, could be neutral researchers because their hair was not being read,[6] I could never occupy a space of neutrality due to the very nature of my position as a black woman. I think that what Martha McCaughey (1997) terms the "relevance of physicality to consciousness" caused me to expect to be read or judged at the bodily level. There was no way that I could escape a reading of my hair among the girls and women I interviewed.

For example, at one point during a very grueling interviewing schedule, I caught a cold, which was complicated by the fact that the weather was also very cold at the time. To prevent myself from getting sicker, I wore hats every time I went outside. One chilly late fall evening, I had an interview with a couple of teens, and before entering their house I forgot to take my hat off. As I began asking the first couple of questions, I noticed that they were looking at my hat. I immediately became aware that my hat was on, with not one single strand showing. I didn't take the hat off entirely. Instead, I shifted it in such a way that I hoped was not too obvious as I attempted to expose my hair. As I suspected, the girls ceased looking at my head. They seemed to have "placed" me, therefore allowing them to move freely into very elaborate and insightful readings of hairstyling practices among black youth.

In other instances, women I interviewed referred to my hair or hairstyle as they addressed particular questions. Whereas Barbara was embarrassed[7] to admit that her brother perceived black women with short, close-cropped hair as masculine, and Mrs. Franklin stated that short hair worn by women made them look masculine, Bobby thought that I looked very feminine with my short hairdo. One of the women confided after I turned the tape off that she wished that she had the courage to cut her hair like mine. These comments demonstrate how my race, gender, and hairstyle affected the women's responses.

In fact, these responses show that the women were quite frank and open in their statements despite, for example, the fact that I wore my hair very short at the time. Along with these comments, other women discussed how short hair is associated with masculinity and being a lesbian. Although Barbara appeared embarrassed in sharing her brother's thoughts, she did not hold back, and Mrs. Franklin displayed no uneasiness whatsoever in stating that women with short-cropped hair had to do much more work in "playing up" their femininity by wearing earrings, makeup, and skirts or dresses. Did the girls tailor their responses based on having "read" my hair after I removed my hat on that very chilly night? Not in the least.

My broader point is to demonstrate that the intersection of race and gender, as well as hairstyle, shaped not only the responses, but also my decision on how to present myself at the bodily level to a certain extent. Indeed, researchers constantly grapple with how to present themselves to their respondents. For example, what attire to wear in particular research settings is an important issue for everyone conducting field research. However, my decision to wear jeans instead of a suit cannot be conflated with my decision to keep my head uncovered as I conducted interviews. Wearing a suit or jeans is not politicized through loaded racialized and gendered discourse, but hair is. Researchers who are not black women would have been able to maintain their position as researcher, but I was able to "transcend" that status because of my race and gender. Although I was the one asking the questions, the black women I interviewed asked me questions as well,[8] used

Appendix I

me as an example in their replies to particular questions, and assumed I would know certain terms used in describing black hair and hairstyling practices.[9] Furthermore, Raine assumed that I knew how to press hair, although if I even look sideways at a pressing comb I swear I can feel the burn on my forehead or ear. In fact, as I attempted to help her press her hair[10] during the interview, she explained that I needed to focus on learning how to *do* black hair instead of writing about it. The expectation that as a black woman I knew all the ins and outs of grooming black women's hair was real.[11] This expectation would not have been placed on other, nonblack female researchers. My position as a researcher was unimportant compared to the loaded implications of my race and gender, and my position as a black woman created certain assumptions.

Thus the time I spent grappling with how I would be perceived based on my hairstyle shaped my actions in the field.[12] Would the *results* of my research have been different had I not been a black researcher? I can't say so for sure, with any assurance, but I don't think that my race afforded me an across-the-board luxury just because I was expected to know certain things. I still had to find ways to ask probing questions without making it look as if I was attempting to separate my position as a black woman from my position as a researcher. No doubt there would have been some moments when followup questions would have been necessary and appropriate regardless of who was doing the interviewing, but because of my race and gender, the girls and women I interviewed *expected* me to know particular terminology and practices associated with hair. Given this expectation, I was both at an advantage and disadvantage as a researcher. I was at an advantage because I was not perceived as an "outsider" or social scientist. But I had never thought about how my race and gender might be a disadvantage. My expectations led me to a less complex understanding of what my field experience would entail. Though it was a great experience, everything was not a bed of roses. I still wonder now how the study would have unfolded if an "outsider" would have been sitting across those tables, sitting on those floors, couches, and steps, asking questions. Would the initial[13] comments have been richer because the girls and women would have felt that they *had* to explain in detail, to someone who is not black and female, why hair matters? Did I ask certain questions that made some of the girls and women uncomfortable because *I am a black woman*? These points are related to my discussion below. How I would be read on the bodily level was also an issue as I asked a particular question during each interview, which ultimately led me to expect some moments of discomfort.

The Expectation and Reality of a Discomfort Zone

"There are some theories that argue that when African American women alter their hair, they are expressing self-hatred? What do you think about that?" One of the most volatile issues concerning black women's hairstyling practices involves hair alteration, particularly straightening one's hair with chemicals, a pressing comb, or a blow dryer. Grier and Cobbs (1968) argue that hair straightening among black women is a sign of self-hatred. By straightening tightly curled or coiled black hair, these psychologists argue, black women are rejecting blackness and embracing white images of beauty. I looked forward to discussing the question of whether such practices are a sign of self-hatred according to the black women I interviewed. But I also approached the question with a certain amount of trepidation.

However, I did not experience the same level of uneasiness in asking the self-hatred question of *all* the women I interviewed. Although I was able to present this question with much ease and comfort to women who wore their hair in "natural styles," this was not the case when I interviewed those with straightened hair. First, I felt uncomfortable because I didn't want the women and girls with straightened hair to think that I favored the self-hatred position. Second, I felt that because I wore my hair in a natural style, the women with straightened hair might again think I supported the self-hatred theory. Finally, despite my understanding that, as a researcher, I wanted the women to grapple with difficult questions, I still wanted somehow to lessen the seeming blow of this question.

As a black woman, I understood the weight of the question and I remembered heated debates about the subject in my own black social circles. My discomfort was not only informed by what I read in the literature, but by my personal experiences. For example, a close friend shared that she was part of a group of black women viewing a film about black women and hair. During the question-and-answer period, one of the women with a natural style explained that she lost a certain amount of respect for black women with straightened hair. Of course, I'm not naive enough to think or even suggest that every black woman wearing natural hairstyles feels that way, but just as straightened hair is politicized within a particular discourse about identity, whether real or imagined, so are natural styles. Furthermore, I felt uneasy because I was dealing not only with my expectation of discomfort among the women I interviewed, but with my own discomfort in having to ask these women with straightened hair this question. My question may not have been a personal question directed at these individual women, but it was a question that involved their personal practices, so in that sense, it was personally loaded. Therefore, I could ask the women with dreadlocks and Afros the question without the feeling that the question had personal connotations, at least at that moment in time.[14]

I could see the discomfort when some of the women rejected the self-hatred accounts of hair alteration by personalizing their responses. Others chuckled as they initially addressed the question, and then commenced to defend black women's rights to adorn their bodies. Several of the women and girls with straightened hair used the opportunity to critique the very thing they were accused of doing: external (whether by those of a different gender and/or race) observations of black women's grooming practices.

Unlike my overall assessment of how my race and gender would be both an advantage and a disadvantage, it was clear to me that being a black woman would definitely be a disadvantage when asking the self-hatred question. I wonder if a nonblack person would have been more at ease in asking such a question of black women who straighten their hair? The discomfort I experienced was not intellectually driven, nor was it *simply* because I felt that I would be offending some of the girls and women. I had been the target of such criticisms when I wore my own hair straightened and this question opened up old wounds that I projected onto the girls and women I interviewed. Though I silently became excited when glaring contradictions surfaced in responses, when that question initially rolled off my lips, I would immediately look for some affirmation on the part of the respondent that she knew that I was not taking a Grier and Cobbs (1968) stance. I can't say for sure exactly what I was hoping to receive: a look, comment, or body gesture? I knew it when I saw it because it was in the way they handled the question. It became clear, interview after interview, that although the question made some of the women uncomfortable, they were not uncomfortable because I was asking it. They were dealing with their own understanding of hair's relationship to racial identity. Because of my race and gender, I was projecting my own discomfort in asking a question that in many ways made me uncomfortable. Therefore, I argue that a nonblack person, and to some extent a black male, would have felt more at ease.

Conclusion

Like my expectations about who would question the value of my work, my race and gender informed my discomfort and expectation of discomfort among some of the girls and women I interviewed regarding the question of self-hatred. Researchers are not perceived equally in the research field; moreover, nor are respondents. If I were conducting the same study with, for example, white women, I would not have had the same expectations that I did in my study with black women. Unlike black women, I would not expect white women to read my hair through an intraracialized discourse. In fact, this would not have been a concern, and I would not have given any thought to wearing a hat during interviews. In addition, the self-hatred question would not have been an issue for white women because self-hatred within the context of hair straightening among blacks relates to a rejection of black physical characteristics and acceptance of white standards of beauty. My understanding about the racial politics of hair are not *only* informed by what I read, but also by personal experiences that are shaped by my race and gender.

I perceive my preoccupation with not wearing hats and wanting to lessen the blow of the self-hatred question to particular respondents as both an advantage and disadvantage. My position demonstrates how black women must continually negotiate race and gender in the research field. It also demonstrates the pitfalls of race-based expectations.

Therefore, researchers should not attempt to avoid race-based expectations. To do so, I argue, allows us to buy into race-blind ideology that erases the difference that race and other dissimilarities among people make in how we see the world. Therefore, if our goal is to conduct studies that do not compromise the lives and perspectives of the people we study as well as our jobs as researchers, then we must grapple with the hard questions and issues that arise in our own conceptualizations as well as those of our respondents. Perhaps my discussion here will lead to further discourse about the "raced" expectations that researchers in general have as we conduct ethnographic or ethnographically informed studies.

Appendix II
Defining Black Hair and Hairstyling Practices

Tables 1 and 2 are based on the operational definitions that I used for grouping the interviewees into categories of "hair types/textures" and "hairstyle." For the present study, "hair types/textures" includes what are commonly known as hairstyles as well as hair textures. I have limited the definition of "hairstyle" in table 2 to length of hair. Table 3 presents popular definitions of black hair terms and hairstyles or hairstyling practices. Although I define terms for my own research purposes in tables 1 and 2, there are important and obvious overlaps between tables 1 and 3.

TABLE 1
Hair Types/Textures

Hair Type/Texture	Definition
Relaxed/permed, straightened/pressed	Chemically and heat altered—straight
Natural	Tightly coiled (a.k.a. "kinky," "nappy"), straight, curly, and/or wavy without chemicals
Braids	Extensions—synthetic or human hair
Dreadlocks	Natural and salon
Weave	Extensions—synthetic or human hair
Chemically altered (other)	Texturizer, jheri curl

TABLE 2

Hairstyles

Hairstyle	Definition
Long	Past shoulders
Medium	Shoulder length
Short	Upper neck/above neck/ cut close to head

TABLE 3

Popular Black Hair and Hairstyling Glossary of Terms

Nappy; kinky; "bad hair": Hair that is tightly coiled or curled. This type of hair is referred to as "natural" black hair because it is not chemically altered. Defined in relationship to "good hair." Although nappy and kinky have derogatory roots that still exist, many blacks have appropriated these terms to describe positive characteristics of tightly coiled or curled black hair. Some natural styles such as the Afro are referred to as nappy or kinky hair.

"Good hair": Hair that is naturally straighter in texture. However, "good" hair can be quite curly but is not tightly coiled or curled such as nappy hair. "Good" hair is defined in relationship to "bad" hair and is perceived as more manageable and desirable.

Natural hair: Hair that is not chemically altered or straightened by the pressing comb or blow dryers. Natural hair and styles are often defined as nappy. They also are associated with black pride and a rejection of white standards of beauty among some blacks.

Relaxed hair; permed hair; relaxer; perm: Hair that is chemically altered, by applying sodium hydroxide (lye) or calcium hydroxide (no lye) to loosen the curl or coil of tightly coiled or curled black hair. As a result, the hair becomes straight after the chemicals are applied. "Relaxer" and "perm" refer to the chemicals or product that is used to straighten the hair. For some blacks, relaxed or permed hair is perceived as rejecting tightly coiled black hair and therefore black physical characteristics.

Pressed hair; straightened hair: Hair that is straightened by heatby using the pressing comb. The pressing comb is also referred to as the "straightening comb" and "hot comb."

Dreadlocks: Hair that is matted together in sections, thereby denoting the term "locks." Has roots in Rastafarianism but many people who wear locks may not be Rastas. However, dreadlocks are associated with black pride for some, and style for others. Some dreadlocks are grown naturally, while others can be sculptured in salons (e.g., silky dreads).

Braids (e.g., micro, box, doo doo, goddess, Bantu knots, Sengalese twists): Synthetic or human hair that is braided into the individual's real hair. This maintains braids for longer periods of time. Braids also allow individuals to wear certain hairstyles (e.g., the bob) and also add length to already existing hair.

Cornrows: Hair braided or twisted in various forms and attached to the scalp.

Plaits: Hair separated in three parts and braided.

Jheri curl: Hair that is chemically altered by applying ammonium thioglyco-late. The hair is then rolled on small rods and dried, leaving the hair curly or wavy. Similar to relaxed or permed hair, the texture of the hair is changed, but the hair is curly and wavy and the curl of the hair does not resemble tightly coiled or curly hair.

Weave: Synthetic or natural hair that is braided, sewn, bonded (i.e., glued), or woven into already existing hair.

Texturized hair; texturizer: Chemically altered hair that can appear straight or curly or way (i.e., like the jheri curl). "Texturizer" is the term that explains the type of chemical that is in the hair.

Note: To ensure the accuracy of the definitions, I asked other black women, some of whom do hair professionally, to review these definitions.

Appendix II

Appendix III
Interviewee Demographics

Alias	Hair Style & Texture	Age	Place of Birth	City Raised	Education Status	Occupation
Elisa	Long: relaxer (straight)	13	Los Angeles	Los Angeles	8th-grade student	Student
Latrice	Long: natural (wavy)	15	Los Angeles	Los Angeles	HS student (sophomore)	Student
Tatiana	Long: natural (straight/wavy/curly)	15	Los Angeles	Los Angeles	HS student (sophomore)	Student
Kai	Long: braid extensions	15	Goleta, CA	Goleta, CA	HS student (sophomore)	Student
Omega	Long: natural (straight)	15	Los Angeles	Santa Barbara, CA	HS student (freshman)	Student
Shanesha	Long: silky dreads	16	Washington, DC	Washington, DC	Continuation school—working on G.E.D.	Student
Grace	Medium: relaxer	16	Norfolk, VA	Atlanta	Junior in HS	Student
Alexis	Long: relaxer	17	Los Angeles	Santa Barbara, CA	HS student (junior)	Student
Jocelyn	Short: relaxer	18	Berkeley, CA	Berkeley, CA	1st-year undergraduate	Student
Lee	Medium: Afro	20	San Francisco	San Francisco	3rd-year undergraduate, Journalism	Student
Ebony	Long: texturizer (straight)	20	Upland, CA	LaVerne & Chico, CA	Undergraduate/ junior, Psych.	Student
Toya	Long: natural (straight & wavy)	20	Grand Rapids, MI	Grand Rapids, MI	Undergraduate/ junior, Political Science	Student
Laurie	Short: natural (close to head)	20	Atlanta	Atlanta	Undergraduate/ junior, English and History	Student
Andaiye	Medium-long: Afro	21	Washington, DC	Military family	Undergraduate/ sophomore (unenrolled)	Dir., After School Program
Crystallina	Long: natural (straight/wavy)	21	Los Angeles	Los Angeles	B.A. in Women's studies	Teacher

(continued)

Alias	Hair Style & Texture	Age	Place of Birth	City Raised	Education Status	Occupation
Cheryl	Short: natural (close to head)	22	New York	Marin, CA	M.S. student, Mechanical Engineering	Graduate student
Semple	Long: natural (wavy)	22	Takoradi, Ghana	Los Angeles	Undergraduate senior, English	Student
Ronnie	Long: braids (extensions)	22	West Covina, CA	Pomona, CA	B.S. in Computer Science	PC Installer
Mercedes	Long: hot comb (straight)	22	Brooklyn, NY	Los Angeles	Undergraduate	Student/ receptionist
Patricia	Long: natural (straight & wavy)	22	Washington, DC	Los Angeles	B.S. in Chemistry	Physician's assistant
Stephanie	Medium: relaxer	22	Oakland, CA	Oakland, CA	HS diploma	Retail/ AFDC
Andrea	Long: hot comb (straight)	24	Oakland, CA	Oakland, CA	Doctoral student, Education	Graduate student
Isha	Long: dreadlocks	24	Washington, DC	DC & San Francisco	4th-year undergraduate	Undergraduate student
Shannon	Medium-long: relaxer	24	Chatanooga, TN	Chatanooga, TN	HS diploma	Housekeeper
Shaquanda	Long: relaxer (straight & wavy)	24	Washington, DC	Los Angeles	B.A. in Theater Arts	Unemployed actress
Elantra	Short: natural (curly)	25	Baton Rouge, LA	Cincinnati	3rd-year doctoral, Bio. Engineering	Graduate student
Keisha	Short-medium: relaxer	25	Minden, LA	Bay Area (Daly City/SF)	M.S.W.	Social worker
Adriana	Long: natural (wavy)	25	San Francisco	San Francisco	2nd-year grad. student, M.S.W.	Graduate student
Lisa	Medium-short: relaxer	25	Atmore, AL	Miami	M.A. grad. student	Graduate student
Stacy	Long: natural (twists)	26	Baltimore	Baltimore	Doctoral student, Anthro.	Graduate student
Ndeye-ante	Long: braids (extensions)	26	New York	NYC & Los Angeles	B.A. in Sociology	Youth Dev. Coordin.
Kim	Long: relaxed	26	Los Angeles	Los Angeles	M.A. in Human Resources Management	Human Resources administrator
Debra	Medium-long: relaxed	27	Berkeley/ Oakland, CA	Berkeley/ Oakland, CA	M.B.A.	Management Consultant
Eve	Long: braids (extensions)	27	Oakland, CA	Oakland, CA	2nd-year grad. student, M.S.W.	Graduate student
Kaliph	Medium-long: relaxer	28	New York	New York	2nd-year doctoral student, Sociology	Graduate student
Indigo	Long: dreadlocks	28	England	Jamaica/Los Angeles	M.A. in Journalism	Ind. Film Maker/ Teacher
Mariya	Short: natural (close to head)	28	Philadelphia	New Jersey	Doctoral student, History	Graduate student

Alias	Hair Style & Texture	Age	Place of Birth	City Raised	Education Status	Occupation
Allison	Short: natural	28	San Diego	San Diego	B.A., Communicative Disorders	Urban Project Dev. Manager
Terri	Short: natural	30	Oakland, CA	Danville, CA	2nd-year grad. student, M.S.W.	Graduate student
Aria	Medium: relaxer	30	Sacramento, CA	Sacramento, CA	Undergraduate/ senior, Black Studies and English	Student
Maxine	Short: relaxer	33	Washington, DC	Washington, DC	10th grade	Unemployed/PA
Charlene	Medium-long: hot comb	33	New York	New York	HS diploma/ some college	Administrative asst.
Sheila	Long: dreadlocks	36	Berkeley/ Oakland, CA	Berkeley/ Oakland, CA	G.E.D./Nursing School	Custom clothing
Esther	Short: perm	37	Washington, DC	Washington, DC	G.E.D.	Unemployed/PA
Jean	Medium-long: natural (wavy/curly)	37	Riverside, CA	All over (military family)	M.A. in Architecture	Architect
Ginger	Short: relaxer	43	Detroit	Los Angeles	M.D.	Physician
Pearl	Short: natural (twists)	45	Bastrop, LA	Bastrop, LA	B.S. in Physical Education	College Counselor
Wixie	Medium: relaxer	45	New Haven, CT/ L.A.	New Haven/L.A.	M.D.	Physician
Mary	Medium-long: French braids	47	Washington, DC	Washington, DC	HS diploma	Unemployed
Asara	Short: natural	47	Louiseville, AR	Louiseville, AR	M.A., Joint Credential in Education	College Counselor
Nia	Short: natural (close to head)	47	Dennison, OH	Uhrichsville, OH	Ph.D. in Educataional Psychology	Director of Res. & Evaluation
Gretchen	Medium-long: relaxer	47	Portsmouth, VA	Portsmouth, VA	M.D.	Physician
Taylor	Short "bobb": relaxer	48	Oakland, CA	Oakland, CA	B.S. in Business Admin.	Accountant
Barbara	Short-medium: relaxed	49	Berkeley, CA	Berkeley, CA	2 years of college college	Asst. II
Ann	Long: relaxer	49	Chicago	At 10 moved to L.A.	University professor	Professor
Raine	Short: hot comb	50	Shreveport, LA	Alameda, CA	HS Diploma	Secretary
Habiba	Short: natural (close to head)	50	Berkeley/ Oakland, CA	Berkeley/ Oakland, CA	M.F.A. in Creative Writing	Writer/ Teacher
Dianne	Short: relaxer	50	Houston	Oakland, CA	Some college	Retired, Material Handler
Dolores	Short: straight (blow dry)	51	Bethesda, MD	Boyds, MD	HS	Unemployed/PA
Mrs. Franklin	Short: hot comb	70	Shreveport, LA	Shreveport, LA	HS diploma	Retired, instructor's assistant
Bobbie	Medium: hot comb	76	Muskogee, OK	Muskogee, OK	B.S. in Home Economics	Retired, clerical

HS = High School
PA = Public Assistance
LPN = License Practical Nurse

61 girls and women combined (individual and focus group interviewees)

Age

Teens = 9
Twenties = 29
Thirties = 7
Forties = 10
Fifties = 4
Seventies = 2

Hairstyles/Types

Relaxer = 22
Natural = 21
Texturizer = 1
Afro = 2
Pressing comb = 5
Blow dry = 1
Dreadlocks = 4
Braids = 4

Education Status

Middle school student = 1
High school student = 7
Did not finish high school = 1
High school diploma/G.E.D. = 7
Associates degree/did not finish
  college = 3
Undergraduate student = 10
M.A. student = 5
Doctoral student = 5
B.A./B.S. = 8
M.A. = 6
Ph.D. = 2
M.D. = 3

Notes

Notes to the Introduction

1. Esi Sagay (1983) also argues that in African societies, hairstyling practices are associated with ceremonial or ritual practices, to denote age, and, like in many other societies, hairstyles also speak to fashion trends. This point is important because Sagay illustrates the importance of viewing hairstyling practices as part of adornment rituals. Hair is just another way of expressing style and fashion, much like clothes, nails, and makeup. In essence, unlike Grier and Cobbs (1968), Sagay argues that hair is very much like a symbolic body of its own that women use for esthetic purposes.

2. Morrow (1973) notes that the comb was carved from wood and the designs were intricate. The comb in African society was designed to accommodate the texture of tightly coiled hair.

3. Morrow (1973) explains how hairstyles were used in competition between tribes. The more lavish the hairstyle, the more prestige bestowed upon tribes and individuals.

4. See Grier and Cobbs (1968).

5. Relaxed is another way of stating "straight." See Appendix II, table 3, for definitions of terms relating to black hair and hairstyles.

6. Also see Rooks's (1996) criticism of Brownmiller's (1984) treatment of "good" hair and "bad" hair.

7. See Butler (1993).

8. Bordo (1993) defines altered bodies as "plastic" bodies.

9. See Lauryn Hill's "Doo Wop (That Thing)," the Fugees' "Nappy Hair," and The Lost Boyz CD, "Love, Peace, and Nappiness."

10. See Paulette Caldwell's (1991) discussion of these cases.

11. One focus-group session was conducted in September 1998.

12. I do not identify which women.

Notes to Chapter 1

1. This is a point that also surfaced in various forms during the focus groups sessions.

2. Through hair.

3. Through internalized notions of beauty.

4. Raine's usage of the term "measly" can also be seen as a generational issue. Raine grew up in the 1950s when hair-care advertisements in black magazines such as *Ebony* and newspapers blatantly castigated tightly coiled black hair. Although the oppressive messages and terminology are subtle today in hair-care advertisements that sell products to African Americans, this was not the case in the 1950s.

5. The most common usage of the term denotes a relationship to measles.

6. Funk and Wagnall's *New Comprehensive International Dictionary of the English Language.*

7. See Morrow (1973); Rooks (1996); and Craig (1997).

8. Many white women fall outside of what is considered beautiful, but it's not because they are *white* women. In contrast when black women fall outside these categories, it is precisely because they are *black* women. In essence, racism and constructions of race are embedded in mainstream notions of beauty, which in general is an advantage for white women because of white privilege and a disadvantage for black women.

9. Charlene used this term to describe the company she works for. In a very general sense, her usage of the term relates to the recognition and celebration of African roots, particularly those within ancient Egypt. See Asante (1988) for a discussion of Afrocentrism and its relationship to ancient Egypt and cultural pride among people of African descent.

1. Madame C. J. Walker invented the straightening comb or pressing comb in 1915.
2. Nia described herself as holding Afrocentric views.
3. This point surfaces later in the chapter.
4. Although Isha does not explicitly note the relationship between spirituality and hair here, she does elsewhere in the interview.
5. In this context, whiteness is used in relationship to mainstream standards of beauty, particularly in relationship to straight hair.

Notes to Chapter 3

1. Per Semple's request.
2. See Memmi's (1965) discussion of how oppressed people take on the beliefs and behavior of the oppressor.
3. Earlier in the interview, Laurie discussed the negative reaction elicited by cutting her hair.
4. Unless they hate their style, as many women often share with friends after a haircut, for example.
5. This is apparent when Semple says, "There isn't very much that we think, say, or do."
6. This was the official newspaper of the United Negro Improvement Association, which Garvey founded in 1916 in Harlem. The masthead of the weekly proclaimed, "A Newspaper Devoted Solely to the Interests of the Negro Race."
7. For example, poor and working-class women, regardless of race, were not viewed as "true women." Those who had to work outside of the home for economic reasons were excluded from the definition of a lady.
8. Not all short hairdos by women, particularly those that resemble traditional men's hairdos (e.g., short-cropped, buzz cuts).
9. For example, both men are "soft spoken" or speak softly, which is a mannerism that is associated with femininity and coyness.

1. Except for the low-income group, which I discuss later in the chapter.
2. I only collected data about parents' occupations from minors.
3. Crystallina's residence at the time of the interview.
4. This was also an issue that surfaced in some of the individual interviews.
5. Similar to Elisa's recognition that she has curlier hair than Tatiana.
6. I also discuss this matter in chapter 4.
7. For example, the image of the Barbie-doll hair.
8. At a birthday party I attended during summer 1997 three girls who were two years old had very long braid extensions in their hair.
9. Ginger is Tatiana's and Elisa's mother.
10. See chapter 1 for Raine's discussion.
11. When it comes to grooming, braids are low maintenance.
12. Passengers can be read as "white."
13. Nevertheless, it is important to note that a physician has power and status that people look up to, whereas a flight attendant does not.
14. See Clarke (1993); Elson (1994); Ayckroyd (1998).

Notes to Chapter 5

1. Such as twists, Bantu knots, close-cropped natural styles, dreadlocks (though locks can be obtained in salons).
2. The Afro has reemerged, especially within the last couple of years.
3. See the music of rap artists such as Public Enemy and the X Clan.
4. Scholars such as Molefi Asante, Donna Richards, C. Tsehloane Keto, Wade Nobles, Asa Hilliard, and Maulana Kerenga, to name a few.

Notes to Appendix I

1. In the case of minors, the location of the interview was determined by parents or guardians.

2. See Appendix II for operational definitions of these terms, as well as classifications that the women fit into based on hair texture and hairstyle.

3. The gap in time was due to the fact that during that timespan I was working on my dissertation, finishing up graduate school, and beginning a position as an assistant professor.

4. See Krieger's (1991) discussion in which she argues that she can no longer write about any subject she studies without reference to her personal involvement. In essence, she rejects the role of the researcher as "neutral" and "objective."

5. I provide a reading of Patricia's question in chapter 4 under the "Early Twenty-Something" focus group session.

6. This is not to suggest that black women do not read or interpret white women's hair or hairstyling practices, but there is a very different reading and interpretive process that occurs within black communities when hair is being read.

7. This was the hairstyle I had at the time, so my reading of Barbara's embarrassment was related to the fact that she had to share her brother's views.

8. See Oakley's (1981) discussion about respondents "asking questions back."

9. For example, many of the women and girls would say, "I don't have to tell you what it means when sistas say that their hair has to be laid before they step out of the house." Indeed, I know that "laid" means your hair has to be done very nicely; however, I would still say what I understood particular terms to mean and the respondents would affirm my statement verbally or by nodding their heads.

10. Per her command, though I was happy to oblige.

11. Granted, I know how to press hair, but according to Raine, my skills were less than stellar. I would agree.

12. For example, not wearing hats during interviews.

13. That is, comments prior to my probing.

14. As my research conveys, many black women have practiced a variety of hairstyling practices in their lifetime.

Notes to Appendix I

References

Asante, Molefi. 1988. *Afrocentricity*. Trenton, N.J.: Africa World Press.

Ayckroyd, Bettina. 1998. "Who Is the Global Ethnic Consumer?" *Cosmetics International* 22 (503) (July 25): 8.

Benton Rushing, Andrea. 1988. "Hair-Raising." *Feminist Studies* 14 (2) (Summer): 325–335.

Berg, Charles. 1951. *The Unconscious Significance of Hair*. London: George Allen and Unwin Ltd.

Berkow, Ira. 1999. "Sprewell Has Golden Opportunity." *New York Times*, February 3, D1.

Bobo, Jacqueline. 1995. *Black Women as Cultural Readers*. New York: Columbia University Press.

Bonner, Lonnie Brittenum. 1991. *Good Hair: For Colored Girls Who've Considered Weaves When the Chemicals Became Too Ruff*. New York: Crown Trade Paperbacks.

Bordo, Susan. 1989. *Gender/Body/Knowledge: Feminist Reconstructions of Knowing*. Newark, NJ: Rutgers University Press.

———. 1993. *Unbearable Weight: Feminism, Western Culture, and the Body*. Berkeley: University of California Press.

Brewer, Rose M. 1993. "Theorizing Race, Class and Gender: The New Scholarship of Black Feminist Intellectuals and Black Women's Labor." In *Theorizing Black Feminisms: The Visionary Pragmatism of Black Women*, Stanlie M. James and Abena P. A. Busia, eds., 13–30. London: Routledge.

Brown, Elaine. 1992. *A Taste of Power: A Black Woman's Story*. New York: Anchor Books, Doubleday.

186   Brownmiller, Susan. 1984. *Femininity*. New York: London Press/Simon and Schuster.

Butler, Judith. 1993. *Bodies that Matter: On the Discursive Limits of "Sex."* New York: Routledge.

Caldwell, Paulette M. 1991. "A Hair Piece: Perspectives on the Intersection of Race and Gender." *Duke Law Journal*, 365–97.

Caraway, Nancie. 1991. *Segregated Sisterhood: Racism and the Politics of American Feminism*. Knoxville: University of Tennessee Press.

Christian, Barbara. 1988. "The Race for Theory." *Feminist Studies* 14 (1): 67–80.

Clarke, Caroline V. 1993. "Redefining Beautiful: Black Cosmetics Companies and Industry Giants Vie for the Loyalty of Black Women." *Black Enterprise,* 23 (11) (June): 242.

Cleage, Pearl. 1993. "Hairpeace: Requirement for Afro-American Women Writers to Discuss Hair." *African American Review* 27 (1) (Spring): 37.

Clemetson, Lynette, and Evan Halper. 1998. "Caught in the Cross-Fire: A Young Star Teacher Finds Herself in a Losing Battle with Parents." *Newsweek*, December 14, 38–39.

Combahee River Collective. 1981. In *This Bridge Called My Back: Writings by Radical Women of Color*, Cherríe Moraga and Gloria Anzaldua, eds., 210–218. New York: Kitchen Table, Women of Color Press.

Cooper, Wendy. 1971. *Hair: Sex, Society, and Symbolism*. New York: Stein and Day.

Craig, Maxine. 1997. "The Decline and the Fall of the Conk; or, How to Read a Process." *Fashion Theory: The Journal of Dress, Body and Culture* 1 (4) (December): 399–419.

Crenshaw, Kimberlé Williams. 1992. "Whose Story Is It Anyway: Antiracist and Feminist Appropriations of Anita Hill." In *Race-ing Justice and En-gendering Power: Essays on Anita Hill, Clarence Thomas, and the Construction of Social Reality*, Toni Morrison, ed., 402–436. New York: Pantheon Books.

Davis, Angela Y. 1994. "Afro Images: Politics, Fashion, and Nostalgia." *Critical Inquiry* 21 (1) (Autumn): 37–45.

Davis, Stephania, and Jerry Thomas. 1996. "Suburban School's Hairdo Ban Tangles with Ethnic Values." *Atlanta Journal\Atlanta Constitution*, November 17, A7.

de Beauvoir, Simone. 1961. *The Second Sex*. New York: Alfred E. Knopf.

de Certeau, Michel. 1984. *The Practice of Everyday Life*. Berkeley: University of California Press.

duCille, Ann. 1996. *Skin Trade*. Cambridge, MA: Harvard University Press.

Eilberg-Schwartz, Howard, and Wendy Doniger, eds. 1995. *Off with Her Head! The Denial of Women's Identity in Myth, Religion, and Culture*. Berkeley: University of California Press.

Elson, Joel. 1994. "Ethnic Cosmetics: Hair Care Gains Are Small, Color Spawns Competition." *Drug and Cosmetic Industry* 155 (5) (November): 24.

Feagin, Joe R., and Melvin P. Sikes. 1994. *Living with Racism: The Black Middle-Class Experience*. Boston: Beacon Press.

Firth, Raymond. 1973. *Symbols: Public and Private*. Ithaca, NY: Cornell University Press.

Freud, Sigmund. 1922. "Medusa's Hair." In *Collected Papers*, 105–106. London: Hogarth Press and the Institute of Psychoanalysis.

Gaskins, Bill. 1996. "Good and Bad Hair." *Chronicle of Higher Education*, October 4, B76.

George, Lynell. 1998. "The Natural Look." *Los Angeles Times*, August 6, E1.

Gibson, Aliona. 1995. *Nappy: Growing Up Black and Female in America*. New York: Harlem River Press.

Giddings, Paula. 1984. *When and Where I Enter: The Impact of Black Women on Race and Sex in America*. New York: Bantam Books.

Gilroy, Paul. 1993. *The Black Atlantic*. London: Oxford University Press.

Golden, Marita. 1983. *Migrations of the Heart*. New York: Ballantine Books.

Goldstein, Laurence. 1991. *The Female Body: Figures, Styles, Speculations*. Ann Arbor: University of Michigan Press.

Grier, William H., and Price M. Cobbs. 1968. *Black Rage*. New York: Basic Books.

Guy-Sheftall, Beverly. 1995. *Words of Fire: An Anthology of African-American Feminist Thought*. New York: New Press.

Hallpike, C. R. 1972. "Social Hair." In *Reader in Comparative Religion: An Anthropological Approach*, William A. Lessa and Evon Z. Vogt, eds., 99–104. New York: Harper and Row.

———. 1987. "Hair." In *Encyclopedia of Religion* 6, Mircea Eliade, ed., 154–157. New York and London: Macmillan.

Herron, Carolivia. 1997. *Nappy Hair*. Illustrated by Joe Cepeda. New York: Alfred A Knopf.

References

188   Hershman, P. 1974. "Hair, Sex, and Dirt." *Man: The Journal of the Royal Anthropological Institute* 9 (2): 274–298.

Hill Collins, Patricia. 1986. "Learning from the Insider Within: The Sociological Significance of Black Feminist Thought." *Social Problems* 33 (6): 14–32.

———. 1989. "The Social Construction of Black Feminist Thought." *Signs: Journal of Women in Culture and Society* 14 (4): 745–773.

———. 1990. *Black Feminist Thought: Knowledge, Consciousness, and the Politics of Empowerment.* London: HarperCollins.

Holloway, Lynette. 1998a. "Teacher in Book Dispute Starts New Job in Queens School." *New York Times,* December 5, B4.

———. 1998b. "Author of Disputed Book Is Criticized in Brooklyn." *The New York Times,* December 9, B13.

———. 1998c. "Unswayed by Debate on Children's Book: Brooklyn Parent Who Stepped Forward Still Dislikes 'Nappy Hair.'" *New York Times,* December 10, B3.

———. 1998d. "Crew Defends Teacher in Book Dispute: Chancellor Says Parents Were Misguided in 'Nappy Hair' Episode." *New York Times,* December 15, B3.

hooks, bell. 1984. *Feminist Theory: From Margin to Center.* Boston: South End Press.

———. 1988. "Straightening Our Hair." *Z Magazine* (Summer): 14–18.

———. 1989. *Talking Back: Thinking Feminist, Thinking Black.* Boston: Beacon Press.

James, Stanlie M., and Abena P. A. Busia. 1993. *Theorizing Black Feminisms: The Visionary Pragmatism of Black Women.* London: Routledge.

Jeter, Tonya, and Denise Crittendon. 1994. "Black Hair: A Crown of Glory and Versatility." *Crisis* 10 (2) (February–March): 7.

Jones, Kelli. 1998. "In the Thick of It: David Hammons and Hair Culture in the 1970s." *Third Text: Third World Perspectives on Contemporary Art and Culture* 44 (Autumn): 17–24.

Jones, Lisa. 1994. *Bulletproof Diva: Tales of Race, Sex, and Hair.* New York: Doubleday.

Kelley, Robin D. G. 1997. "Nap Time: Historicizing the Afro." *Fashion Theory: The Journal of Dress, Body and Culture* 1 (4) (December): 339–351.

———. 1998. *Yo Mama's Disfunktional!: Fighting the Culture Wars in Urban America.* Boston: Beacon Press.

Krieger, Susan. 1991. *Social Science and the Self.* New Brunswick, NJ: Rutgers University Press.

Leach, Edmund R. 1958. "Magical Hair." *Journal of the Royal Anthropological Institute* 88: 147–164.

Leyden, Liz. 1998. "N.Y. Teacher Runs Into a Racial Divide." *Washington Post*, December 3, A3.

Little, Benilde. 1996. *Good Hair: A Novel.* New York: Simon and Schuster.

Litwack, Leon F. 1961. *North of Slavery: The Negro in the Free States, 1790–1860.* Chicago: University of Chicago Press.

Mageo, Jeannette M. 1994. "Hairdos and Don'ts: Hair Symbolism and Sexual History in Samoa." *MAN* 29 (2) (June): 407.

McCaughey, Martha. 1997. *Real Knockouts: The Physical Feminism of Women's Self-Defense.* New York: New York University Press.

Memmi, Albert. 1965. *The Colonizer and the Colonized.* Boston: Beacon Press.

Mercer, Kobena. 1990. "Black Hair/Style Politics." In *Out There: Marginalization and Contemporary Cultures*, Russell Ferguson, et al., eds., 247–264. New York and Cambridge, U.K.: New Museum of Contemporary Art and MIT Press.

Morgenstern, Julian. 1966. "The Sacrifice of Hair." In *Rites of Birth, Marriage, Death and Kindred Occasions among the Semites*, 84–104. Cincinnati: Hebrew Union College Press.

Morrow, Willie. 1973. *400 Years without a Comb.* San Diego: Black Publishers of San Diego.

Moynihan, Daniel Patrick. 1965. "The Tangle of Pathology." In *The Black Family: Essays and Studies*, Robert Staples, ed., 5–14. Belmont, CA: Wadsworth Publishing.

Nelson, Jill. 1997. *Straight, No Chaser: How I Became a Grown-up Black Woman.* New York: Penguin Books.

———. 1998. "Stumbling upon a Race Secret." *New York Times*, November 27.

Norsworthy, Kym. 1991. "Hair Discovery." *Real News* 2 (1): 3, 8.

Oakley, Ann. 1981. "Interviewing Women: A Contradiction in Terms." In *Doing Feminist Research*, Helen Roberts, ed. London: Routledge and Kegan Paul.

Obeyesekere, Gananath. 1981. *Medusa's Hair: An Essay on Personal Symbols and Religious Experience.* Chicago: University of Chicago Press.

References

190   Ogunnaike, Lola. 1998. "Some Hair Is Happy to be Nappy." *New York Times*, December 28, B11.

Okazawa-Rey, Margo, et al. 1986. "Black Women and the Politics of Skin Color and Hair." *Women's Studies Quarterly 14*, 1 and 2 (Spring/Summer): 13–14.

Omi, Michael, and Howard Winant. 1984. *Racial Formation in the United States: From the 1960s to the 1980s*. New York: Routledge.

Patterson, Orlando. 1982. *Slavery and Social Death: A Comparative Study*. Cambridge, MA: Harvard University Press.

Peterson-Lewis, Sonja. 1994. "Aesthetic Practices Among African American Women." In *The African Aesthetic: Keeper of Traditions*, Kariamu Welsh Asante, ed., 103–141. New York: Greenwood Press.

Reid, Calvin. 1998. "'Nappy Hair' Flap Spurs Book Sales." *Publishers Weekly*, December 7, 16.

Reilly, Nick. 1998. "Counter Point." *Sports Illustrated*, March 9, 82–93.

Roberts, Dorothy. 1997. *Killing the Black Body: Race, Reproduction, and the Meaning of Liberty*. New York: Pantheon Books.

Rooks, Noliwe. 1996. *Hair Raising: Beauty, Culture, and African American Women*. New Brunswick, NJ: Rutgers University Press.

Rose, Tricia. 1994. *Black Noise: Rap Music and Black Culture in Contemporary America*. Hanover, NH: Wesleyan University Press.

Russell, Midge, et al. 1992. *The Color Complex: The Politics of Skin Color among African Americans*. New York: Harcourt Brace Jovanovich.

Sagay, Esi. 1983. *African Hairstyles: Styles of Yesterday and Today*. Oxford: Heinemann International Literature and Textbooks.

St. Jean, Yanick, and Joe R. Feagin. 1998. *Double Burden: Black Women and Everyday Racism*. Armonk, NY: M. E. Sharpe.

Shipp, E. R. 1988. "Are Cornrows Right for Work?" *Essence*, February, 109–110.

Sikes, E. E., and Louis H. Gray. 1928. "Hair and Nails." *Encyclopedia of Religion and Ethics* 6: 474–477.

Tyler, Bruce M. 1990. "Black Hairstyles: Cultural and Socio-political Implications." *Western Journal of Black Studies* 14 (4): 235–250.

Wade Gayles, Gloria. 1993. "The Making of a Permanent Afro." In *Pushed Back to Strength: A Black Woman's Journey Home*, 133–158. Boston: Beacon Press.

Walker, Alice. 1988. "Oppressed Hair Puts a Ceiling on the Brain." In *Living by the Word*, 69–74. Orlando, FL: Harcourt Brace Jovanovich.

White, Shane, and Graham White. 1998. *Stylin': African American Expressive Culture from Its Beginnings to the Zoot Suit*. Ithaca, NY, and London: Cornell University Press.

Wing, Katherine A. 1997. *Critical Race Feminism: A Reader*. New York University Press.

Wolfe, George C. 1987. "The Hairpiece." In *The Colored Museum*, 19–23. New York: Broadway Play Publishing.

References

Index

adornment practices: as cultural artifacts, 8, 122; as empowering for blacks, 27–28, 64–65; and self-hatred, 55–56, 65; of young girls, 121–22, 135–36

advertising: and nappy hair, 24; about tightly coiled hair, in the 1950s, 180n. 4; at the turn of the nineteenth century, 11

Afro: and identity politics, 10–11, 86; and law enforcement, 15–16; political meaning of, 15, 124–27

Afrocentrism, 40, 45, 140; and ancient Egypt, 180n. 9

age: and awareness of hair, 135–36; impact on choice of hairstyle, 83. *See also* girls, hairgrooming practices of; senior women, hairgrooming practices of; teenagers

Ally McBeal (tv program), 129

alteration of hair: for economic success, 62–63; and empowerment, 51, 63; emulating whiteness, 10, 61–62, 63; for expedience, 51; as experimentation, 50; as expression of independence, 49–50; as expression of self-love, 64–65; impact of tradition on, 54; and insecurity, 65; and intent, 48–49; for manageability, 49, 60; and mating choices, 59; as personal choice, 52–53, 67, 134–35; practical reasons for, 46–47; and self-hatred, 8–10, 12, 43–59, 167–69; and socialization in America, 51–52

American Airlines, 16, 81

Artist, The, 94, 95

assimilationists, views about hairstyling practices, 8

"bad hair": definition of, 2, 12–13; racial contexts of, 12–13; and self-esteem of children, 118; social meanings of, 28–31, 77. *See also* nappy hair

beauty: black men's perceptions of, 9, 34, 59, 78, 96–97; and black women, 10–12, 30, 86, 120; as normalizing discipline, 23; self-definition of, 86; social concepts of, 82, 180. *See also* standards of beauty, mainstream

beauty salons: black professional women's use of, 130–33; as institution of socialization in black communities, 130–33

Berg, Charles, 5

Black Atlantic, The (Gilroy), 146

"Black Hair/Style Politics" (Mercer), 8, 122

"Black Hairstyles: Cultural and Socio-political Implications" (Tyler), 8

black popular culture, 35–36

Black Power movement, 124, 127

Black Rage (Grier and Cobbs), 9, 43

black womanhood, constructions of, 75, 79, 87

Bobo, Jacqueline, 11

body, perceptions of women about, 68, 81–82

Bone, Krayzie, 95

Bordo, Susan, 13, 23, 26

braids: definition of, 172; employment policies about, 16; as expression of a black esthetic, 17; school policies concerning, 16

Bristol, Carlos, 2

About the Author

Ingrid Banks is Assistant Professor of Black Studies at Virginia Tech. She received her B.A. in U.S. History and her Ph.D. (1997) in Ethnic Studies (Social Science emphasis) from the University of California, Berkeley. Banks's main research area is African American Studies with an emphasis on the intersection of race, gender, and class. Her research also focuses on race and racism within the United States, black popular culture, black feminist theory, critical race theory, teaching methods, and qualitative research methods. Banks's essay "Resistance in Three Acts: Ideological and Practical Implications" appears in a recent special issue of the journal *Feminist Teacher* that examines resistance in teaching. She is also the author of an op-ed article, "Reliance on Technology Threatens the Essence of Teaching," in the October 16, 1998, issue of the *Chronicle of Higher Education*.

RENNER LEARNING RESOURCE CENTER
ELGIN COMMUNITY COLLEGE
ELGIN ILLINOIS 60123